A Practical Guide to

Facilitation

Skills

A Practical Guide to
Facilitation Skills

A Real - World Approach

**TONY SPINKS AND
PHIL CLEMENTS**

**KOGAN
PAGE**

First published in 1993

Kogan Page Limited
120 Pentonville Road
London N1 9JN

© Tony Spinks and Phil Clements, 1993

British Library Cataloguing in Publication Data
A CIP record for this book is available from the British Library
ISBN 0 7494 1003 5

Typeset by Books Unlimited (Nottm) – Sutton-in-Ashfield, NG17 1AL
Printed and bound in Great Britain by Biddles Ltd, Guildford and King's Lynn

Contents

Acknowledgements

I am very grateful to my dad Keith, who spent many long evenings reading and editing this book, and, in the process, helped us knock it into some kind of shape. I would also like to thank Jane, my wife, for her constant support during a project which took up so much of my time. I have gained a great deal from working alongside many dedicated and skilled facilitators; of these, I would particularly like to mention Guy Hewlett and Richard Griggs, with whom my interest in and approach to facilitation developed, and also Laurie Trott, who inspired my thinking and facilitation in so many ways.

TS

My thanks go to Dr James Kilty, who sowed the seeds of my interest in facilitation; Professor Duncan Harris of Brunel University, who gave us advice about writing a book; to Chris Edwards, who debated the issues with me and listened; but mostly to my wife Heather, who has supported and encouraged me throughout this project.

PC

Introduction

We have been involved in the facilitation of adult learning for many years, working in the areas of equal opportunities and fair treatment, assertiveness, personal development, team-building and interpersonal skills. Facilitators are essentially enablers or encouragers of learning who seek to achieve this by focusing on the experiences and activity of the learner, unlike the more traditional didactic methods of teaching which have tended to be the main experience of learners in our schools, colleges, high schools and other establishments where training and education take place.

Our experience has shown us that, to be successful, facilitation must promote *relevant* learning which is of use to the learners in the real world of their everyday lives. Facilitation must also be *seen* to do this, not only by learners attending facilitated training courses, but also by those who arrange and sponsor these courses.

- **Learners** need to believe that facilitation can and will promote learning which is relevant, significant and meaningful to them and which will be of use to them in everyday situations, such as in the workplace.
- **New trainers** need to see that facilitation can encourage learning in a training environment, that will become translated into action or necessary change by students because of its relevance to their real world.
- **Sponsors and managers** of training need to know that facilitation promotes learning which lasts far beyond the immediate training sessions they have sanctioned. Like it or not, we are now in an era of enterprise education, cost-centring, market testing and, above all, value for money. Training is expensive, and it must prove its worth by adopting a pragmatic

9

approach which encourages learning that is readily transferable to and helpful in dealing with real-world problems and situations.

- **Experienced facilitators** (as enablers of learning) require, more than ever, an approach which places issues of learner relevance, significance and meaning at the very centre of their facilitation.

Members from each of these groups on both sides of the Atlantic will find this book of value because it offers practical and accessible advice and ideas on maximizing the relevance and thus the effectiveness of learning achievable within a training environment.

Each of us lives and works in the real world of everyday life. To be fully effective, facilitation must reflect this fact by being systematically tailored to meet its demand and account for its realities. Learners bring experiences of their real world into the learning environment and all too often this is ignored. Likewise, learning achieved in the classroom or other learning setting must become more applicable to, and of use in, the everyday world of the learner if it is to be considered successful and worthwhile.

These issues when taken together, point to the need for a new, more realistic approach to facilitation. This book answers that need by offering a training model that systematically addresses these vital factors at each stage of the facilitative process. To capture the essence of this timely new approach we have called it *Real-world Facilitation*.

CHAPTER 1

Real-world Facilitation Explained and Compared

Outline

In this chapter the concept of Real-world Facilitation will be explained in some detail. As a distinct approach to facilitation, the model is then compared with other major approaches to training with which you may be familiar. The chapter also encourages you to identify the way you facilitate now, providing an opportunity for you to reflect on the effectiveness of your approach in light of the questions about meaningful learning raised throughout the chapter.

Planned learning outcomes

By the time you have read through this chapter you should have a clearer understanding of:

- *What Real-world Facilitation is.*
- *How it builds upon and complements current methods of facilitation.*

- *How its application will encourage meaningful learning for your students.*
- *Your own facilitative style.*
- *How Real-world Facilitation differs from current methods of facilitation.*

WHAT REAL-WORLD FACILITATION IS

What would you like this book to be like? Spend a few moments thinking about what, in an ideal world, this book should offer you as a practical guide ... what are your expectations of a book on facilitation?

Having asked our own colleagues their views as to what would constitute a good book on facilitation, many of them suggested things like; 'It ought to be interesting', 'It should be relevant to my work', 'It should be of use to me', 'It should be written in a way that I can understand and should be easy to get into', 'It should be significant, building on my existing knowledge and offering me something new'. In short it should be:

Relevant
Useful
Significant
Interesting
Meaningful
Realistic
Useable
Helpful

It is quite likely that these factors will be important to you too. Few people will be inclined to spend time working through a book which is difficult to read, lacks meaning and relevance, seems to talk in another language and doesn't offer useful and useable advice ... especially if that book claims to be a practical guide to encouraging meaningful learning.

Let's change direction slightly now, and instead of thinking about what you hope to find in this book, imagine perhaps that you are a learner about to attend a facilitated training course. Having received a course outline and timetable, you will no doubt begin to form expectations of what the course might offer you and what it might be like. You may also hope for a particular type of facilitator, skilled and willing to encourage and support your learning.

Interestingly, and perhaps not surprisingly, the very things that you hope this book will offer you are in fact the very things that you, as a student, would benefit most from in the classroom (and in other training environments as well). In short, facilitated learning, like a good book, should be *relevant, significant* and *meaningful* to the learner if it is to be effective and long-lasting.

It would be useful here to take a quick look at our leading principle, the elements of which have already been touched upon in the opening part of this chapter.

The Leading Principle of Real-world Facilitation

Learning should be relevant, significant and meaningful to the learner *at every stage* of the facilitative process. It should make sense and be of use in the learner's real world.

A good way to understand the impact of this model is to think of it as providing a bridge for the learner between the training environment and the real world of lived experience; this is illustrated in Figure 1.1. By systematically applying the principles of Real-world Facilitation to every stage of the training process you will be able to offer your learners a bridge between:

Learning from activities and group work, undertaken in a training setting	$\longrightarrow$	The real-world contexts within which that learning will be put into practice
Experiences that occur within the learning group	$\longrightarrow$	The wider experiences of the learner's everyday world

In respect of your own approach to facilitating learning, the model will provide you, the facilitator, with a bridge between:

Theories about facilitation and experiential learning	$\longrightarrow$	Your facilitation in practice (planning, delivery and committing learners to future action)

At the point of course delivery when you are facilitating learning with a group of learners, this approach will also enable you to encourage them to cross each learning bridge, by working through the process of understanding and interpreting what they have learned in the training session in terms of its consequences for, and impact on, their real world (for example the workplace).

Let's look at an example of how this might work in practice. An important aspect of equal opportunities training is the need to develop each learner's ability and commitment to challenging colleagues who exhibit inappropriate

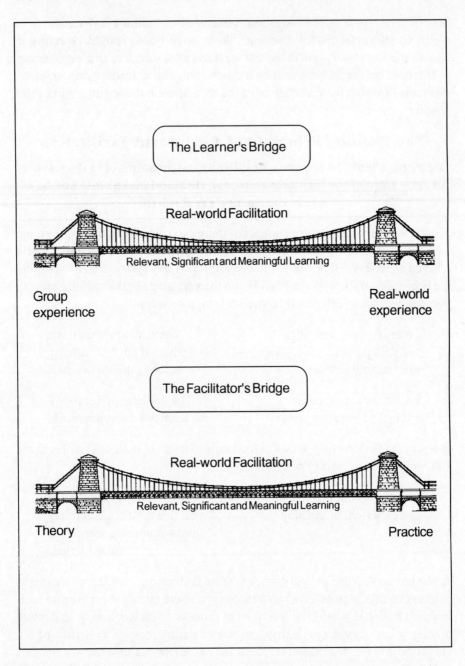

The Learner's Bridge

Real-world Facilitation

Relevant, Significant and Meaningful Learning

Group
experience

Real-world
experience

The Facilitator's Bridge

Real-world Facilitation

Relevant, Significant and Meaningful Learning

Theory

Practice

Figure 1.1 *Two ways in which Real-world Facilitation provides a learning bridge*

attitudes and behaviour in the workplace. When we run such courses we invite our learners to devise strategies for making appropriate challenges in such situations.

Learning about the different ways of confronting and challenging within the safe learning environment of the classroom is certainly important, but learners need to think through the real-world consequences of such challenges. How realistic are such strategies and how confident is the learner to use them? How confident is the learner to use certain challenges? What is the point of developing types of challenging which are either ineffective or will never be used? To answer these questions the learner needs to be encouraged to both see and establish the necessary links between what is being suggested in a training setting and its actual implications for the real world, where learning should become translated into action or change. Learners need to be encouraged to cross the bridge.

Later in this chapter we will compare this new model of facilitation with other major approaches to training with which you may be familiar. First, however, it is important that we take time to describe in some detail other key aspects of Real-world Facilitation.

Pause for Thought

- *As you read through each point, think about the similarities and differences that exist between Real-world Facilitation and your own approach to facilitating learning.*
- *If you are new to facilitation, try to compare our approach with methods and styles of encouraging learning you may have read about or observed others using.*

KEY ASPECTS OF THE REAL-WORLD FACILITATION MODEL

Real-world Facilitation:

- Depends on a *systematic approach* to facilitation which takes account of the ways in which each phase of the facilitative process can influence learning outcomes. For example, the choice of learning activities during the planning phase of any course can directly influence learner involvement at the point of course delivery.
- It requires the facilitator to consider and maximize the *relevance* of

learning at the planning, delivery and future action phases of the facilitative process. For example, does the training link into aspects of the learners' real world – the jobs they do, the roles they perform, their backgrounds, etc? (Note: The future action phase is the point(s) during a course at which learners are encouraged to begin the process of transforming learning into possible future action.)

- It encourages learning that is *significant* for the learner by demanding that the facilitator fully considers whether the structure and content of the training course is at an appropriate level. That is to say, the training session should facilitate personal development in the area being addressed, taking the learner beyond what he or she knows already by offering new information and new ways of looking at or understanding existing attitudes, values or behaviour.
- It requires that learning should be *meaningful* to the learner. It should make sense and be understandable. This requires that the facilitator should help the learner to establish the necessary links between the training context where learning is introduced and the context of everyday life (the workplace, for example) within which any learning will become translated into action or necessary change by the learner.
- It fully embraces the central features of facilitated learning, building upon styles of training which are *learner-centred, experiential,* offer freedom to learn and which encourage *learning-through-doing.*
- It acknowledges the importance of the ongoing learning process in which learners become involved, whilst *refocusing* and *redirecting* that process *as necessary*, to ensure that it remains relevant, significant and meaningful to the learner.
- It *directs learning* towards identified and appropriate learning outcomes which themselves reflect both organizational and individual learning needs.
- It is based upon the idea of a *partnership* between facilitator and learner such that encouragement to learn is properly directed to realize planned learning outcomes (you may call these aims and objectives or learning intentions).
- It is *purposeful* in that it seeks to promote learner commitment to necessary individual and organizational change.
- It is *responsive*, acknowledging that initial course plans and anticipated learning outcomes need to be flexible, so as to allow learners to participate in directing their own learning.
- It keeps the *distinction* between the world of the learning group and the

learner's real world in view, while constantly trying to provide a bridge between the two for the learner.

- It is *challenging*, where this is necessary to encourage learners to reflect upon the validity and appropriateness of both their disclosed and undisclosed attitudes and values, in terms of real-world consequences.
- It encourages learners to question for themselves the validity and appropriateness of both their declared and undeclared attitudes and values in terms of *real-world consequences*.

Each of these points will be dealt with in greater detail within the chapter which deals with that stage of the facilitative process. To illustrate the main points provided in this list we have created a mind-map (see Figure 1.2). This graphical method of notation and brainstorming was developed by Tony Buzan (1989) and it provides a powerful method of charting ideas and their relationships.

CLARIFYING YOUR CURRENT APPROACH

When you want to clarify for yourself where you stand on a particular point or issue, it can sometimes be very helpful to work out what the two most extreme positions on that issue might be, imagining a line drawn between these opposite 'ends' as representing a range of alternative positions. By forcing yourself to choose whereabouts on this line you actually stand, you will make it clear in your own mind what your position on that issue currently is.

Figure 1.3 provides a good worked example of this idea by describing a range of educational opposites. Your position on the lines which link each pair of extreme positions will suggest aspects of your approach to facilitating learning.

Pause for Thought

Take a moment to reflect on the educational opposites in Figure 1.3, relating them to your own experience. If you are new to this area, try and imagine the type of facilitation that you will become involved with.

- *Where would you place yourself in each case?*
- *Is your position on the line where you want to be?*
- *To what extent might a position to the right or to the left of centre suggest a particular facilitative style or approach?*

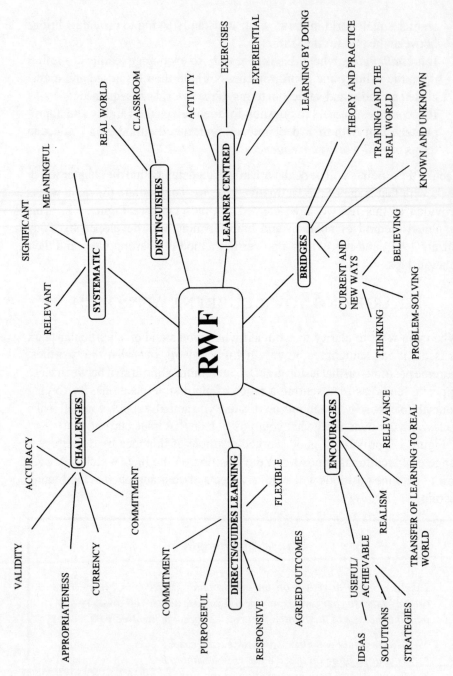

Figure 1.2 *Some of the characteristics of Real-world Facilitation*

If your experiences are similar to ours, you may well have come to the conclusion that the educational positions described at the right-hand ends of the
scales in each case are interrelated and even feed off each other; the same is
also true of the other extreme. For example, a person-centred trainer or facilitator might also be labelled as 'laid back', process-oriented, syllabus-free, etc.
On the other hand, an authoritative teacher might also be seen as directive,
product-oriented, linear and syllabus-bound.

In terms of Real-world Facilitation we believe that if, as a trainer, you place
yourself at or near one or other of these extremes, you are in very real danger
of falling into one of the following traps:

- At the directive/product-oriented extreme, learner needs tend to be
  assumed by the facilitator, who pre-plans and then imposes a learning
  structure upon learners. This is a 'facilitator-knows-best' view, whereby
  the choices of exercises and materials tend not to reflect the learners' own
  issues and concerns; having been chosen before the event, they are then
  doggedly adhered to. Here the *facilitator's* view of what is relevant,
  significant and meaningful takes precedence over the learners'.
- At the process-oriented/syllabus-free extreme, the group process itself
  becomes the main agenda. Learning outcomes become decided almost
  on-the-spot as interactions between group members suggest new direc-
  tions for the group to move in. No links with real-world experience or
  real-world contexts are made, leaving learners to make sense of what they
  have experienced for themselves. There can be a lack of clear direction in
  the group and this may generate learner frustration and the devaluation of
  the learning process.

We do accept that these descriptions of two facilitative extremes are somewhat
stereotypical. That is not to say that they do not exist at all; we have direct
experience of teaching styles which fall easily into one or other of these
approaches.

As a facilitator you will often be in the position of controlling the learning
process for your learners, deciding the direction that such learning should take,
the exercises and activities that your learners should participate in and the level
and manner in which they should interact with you and with each other.
Because of this, it is extremely important that you should establish an accurate
idea of your facilitative style and think about the influence and effect that your
approach has on your learners and their learning.

During the last *pause for thought* section you were encouraged to identify
where you stood in respect of a series of educational opposites. The results of

Education ————————	Training
Learner-Centred ————————	Teacher-Centred
Freedom ————————	Authority
Process ————————	Product
Facilitative ————————	Didactic
Laid back ————————	Authoritarian
Non-directive ————————	Directive
Person-Centred ————————	Task-Centred
Wholeness ————————	Fragmentation
Syllabus-Free ————————	Syllabus-bound
Interconnected ————————	Linear
Divergent thinking ————————	Convergent thinking
Experience-based ————————	Information-based

Figure 1.3 *Some educational opposites. Where do* you *stand?*

this exercise will provide you with a profile of your current facilitative approach. Keep this in mind as you read through the next part of this chapter.

OTHER MODELS OF FACILITATION

Much of our work, and therefore the context in which our thinking about facilitation has developed, has been in the areas of equal opportunities, fair treatment, interpersonal skills, quality of service delivery and the adoption of organizational values. We have worked with people from both the public and the private sectors, although our main work has been with police officers, police civilian employees, police trainers and police recruits (police learners undertaking their first 20 weeks of training).

In our experience, facilitation methods currently being used within the field of equal opportunities and fair treatment training and within the area of interpersonal skills training (which includes team-building, assertiveness and quality-of-service training) tend to be one of three broad types. We have chosen to categorize these facilitation styles as *intervention analysis*, *neutral facilitation* and *mechanical facilitation* (see Figure 1.4); you may be familiar with them under different names.

INTERVENTION ANALYSIS

This approach acknowledges that sensitive facilitation skills are transferable between the learning, counselling and therapeutic environments. Described by John Heron in such works as *Six Category Intervention Analysis* (1989), *Dimensions of Facilitator Style* (1977) and *The Facilitator's Handbook* (1989), this approach seeks to raise the facilitator's awareness of the effect that certain ways of intervening in group learning have on individual group members.

By understanding the consequences for the learning process of intervening in certain ways, the facilitator can direct and encourage particular learning outcomes. Specific types of intervention tend to invite particular responses from learners. For example, if the facilitator wants a learner to think about the validity of an attitude or behaviour they are displaying, then he or she may choose to employ a confronting intervention: 'I notice that whenever a member of the group starts to talk about their feelings, Derek, you sigh and raise your eyes to the ceiling. Why do you do that?' etc. Other interventions might include a 'directive intervention' (the facilitator chooses to direct the group in some way), an 'interpretative intervention' (the facilitator attempts to make sense of what is happening in the group) and so on.

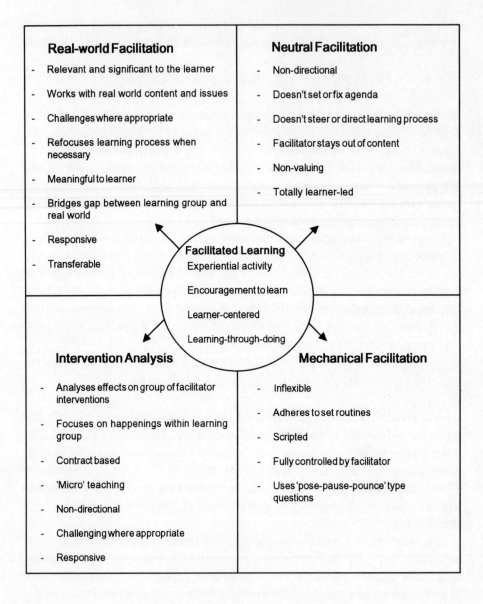

Figure 1.4 *A model of main facilitative styles*

Intervention analysis, if used skilfully, is a valuable means of monitoring the way you work with groups and individuals and can raise your awareness of the effects that you, as the facilitator, are having on the learning process. We have worked with intervention analysis for nearly five years, threading it into our facilitative style with a view to intervening in the learning process in a more sensitive, aware and effective manner.

Our successes with this method of facilitation have been many, but at the same time, we have also become aware of its limitations, particularly in terms of its scope for encouraging meaningful learning. Its point of focus tends to be fixed on happenings within the learning group, thereby amplifying the group process and group dynamics to the point at which these things begin to take over the agenda. Terms and phrases used by the facilitator to intervene in group learning can appear unreal and insincere: 'How did that make you feel?'; 'What's happening for you right now?'; 'Would you share that with the group?', etc. Courses are characterized by detailed contract setting which often has the undesired side-effect of raising learner anxiety unnecessarily and exercises leave learners with the task of making the links with their own real world for themselves. Taken together, these aspects of intervention analysis suggest that it is a form of 'micro-teaching' which, although offering valuable 'tools' to the facilitator, fails to place learner-relevance, significance and meaningful learning where we believe they ought to be: centre stage.

NEUTRAL FACILITATION

As its name suggests, this is an approach in which the facilitator becomes an uninvolved and neutral guide, a person who helps the group through their pre-set agenda without offering opinion or placing value on the group's findings. The neutral facilitator will not channel the group's efforts in any particular direction but will instead identify alternatives and facilitate group decisions on the best way to move forward. Where necessary, the facilitator will reflect back to the group its findings and decisions to date and any indication that it has lost its way; it then remains a matter for the group as how best to refocus the efforts of its members. In this sense neutral facilitation is totally learner-led.

The facilitator must stay out of the content of the various learning stages at all times but may, where appropriate, offer methods of achieving learning outcomes that have been agreed as desirable by the group members themselves. There must be a clear indication of the exact nature of the facilitator's role at the outset of the session and this role should be clarified during the learning process itself, if clarification is required. Movement out of the facilitative 'neutral zone' should ideally be negotiated with and agreed by the group.

In any sphere of adult, learner-centred training, a method which invites learners to work through problems for themselves is of value. Neutral facilitation has this strength, shifting a great deal of the responsibility for learning onto the learner, who, with the help of a friendly guide, might benefit from the freedom of totally learner-directed learning. With careful and considered use such benefits are possible.

We have used neutral facilitation many times and in many different situations with mixed success. If used sparingly, as one of a number of facilitation tools, rather than as a distinct approach in its own right, it can encourage greater learner autonomy and lessen the effect of facilitator interference where this is felt to be a problem. The down-side is that learners often become frustrated by the lack of direction offered by the facilitator and find the learning group incapable of making necessary process decisions. Agreed agendas tend to be shallow, avoiding the real issues, or else unrealistically optimistic. It becomes all too easy for the group to lose its way, despite the best efforts of the facilitator. Competing learning needs amongst group members may also interfere with the establishment of agreed learning outcomes.

The overarching difficulty is that, in fact, neutrality is not achievable. For example, when facilitating equal opportunities, the learners *know* you are not neutral but are in favour of fairness and against racism and sexism, yet they see you pretending to be otherwise.

> If we are to wear the mantle of (educator), we must, at some minimum level, make explicit the criteria by which we determine the educational worth of our efforts. ... Not to do so is unthinking or dishonest and it is to consign ourselves to being adaptive and reactive satisfiers of whatever consumer learning needs happen to capture our attention (Brookfield, 1991).

MECHANICAL FACILITATION

When an individual starts out as a facilitator, the skills required to effectively enable group learning often seem daunting, unnatural and unachievable, despite appearing deceptively natural and easy in the hands of a skilled facilitator. Each of us has been in this position, as we try to grapple with such aspects of training as self-confidence, questioning techniques, spread of eye-contact, use of hand gestures, silence, time-management, flexibility, etc.

In these early days, trainers are often encouraged to adopt step-by-step routines (following a carefully prepared lesson plan for example) which enable them to acquire experience whilst ensuring an acceptable level of delivery for their learners. During this time the facilitator is acutely aware of his or her own presence and activities within the group and will probably stick to a form of pre-planned script as a form of lifeline. It is this methodical, deliberate and self-aware approach to facilitation which we have termed 'mechanical facilitation'.

Meaningful learning is obviously difficult in such circumstances. Anticipated learning outcomes are likely to have been pitched at a level considered 'achievable' by the facilitator, so they are unlikely to take account of the learner's self-identified learning needs. Mechanical facilitation is characterized by a high degree of inflexibility and adherence to set routines, giving the impression that it has been rehearsed or practised. Because of this there is a high degree of facilitator control, as deviation from the lesson plan may well leave the facilitator vulnerable, exposed and found wanting; at least, this is the fear.

It is not only those who are new to facilitation who may adopt a mechanical approach to their work. Those who fear the consequences of transferring responsibility for learning to their learners (believing that a loss of trainer control will result), may also be tempted to adopt such an approach in an effort to maintain their authority.

Pause for Thought

Take a few moments to look at Figure 1.4 which outlines these different types of facilitation.

- *Can you identify aspects of your own facilitation style in the categories shown?*
- *Have you tried a style of facilitation which hasn't worked for you? If so, what were the reasons for this?*

The various shortcomings of *intervention analysis*, *neutral facilitation* and *mechanical facilitation* that we have identified above, although different, all arise because, in one respect or another and despite adhering to the basic concepts of facilitation, each fails to start from and systematically maintain a fundamental commitment towards ensuring that *learning is relevant, significant and meaningful to the learner **at every stage** of the facilitative process, and that it makes sense and is of use in the learner's real world.*

The process of interpreting the meaning, relevance and significance of new information, of capturing its essence and implications, requires that the learner should access his or her existing stock of knowledge and beliefs, ideas and values and that he or she should reflect upon their past experiences, using these as the tools by which such new information is rendered intelligible and meaningful. In the course of learning, the learner must bring to bear upon new ideas and new problems, existing ways of thinking, testing, understanding, organizing and validating and through this integrative process of comprehension and comparison, he or she will create new ways of thinking and understanding and new meaning.

It follows that effective and long-lasting learning can best be encouraged by adopting an approach which acknowledges and draws upon the learner's existing knowledge, skills and experiences, using these as a backdrop against which new information will become understood and its meaning distilled (Ausubel et al, 1978; Schutz, 1962; 1964; 1966). As you will see, these are key ideas which underpin the Real-world Facilitation model.

Having provided you with an explanation of Real-world Facilitation in this opening chapter, it's now time to invite you to stay with us for a more detailed exploration of what we believe is a timely and much needed change of direction in facilitation.

CHAPTER 2

Real-world Facilitation Principles

Outline

In the first chapter we explained the concept of Real-world Facilitation, providing you with a fairly broad outline of the model and comparing it with other methods of facilitation.

This chapter will develop that theme by looking at Real-world Facilitation in closer detail and by setting out some important principles. It will also lead you into the use of these principles in such areas as the choice of facilitation style, learning exercises and other materials. In short, it will provide you with an at-a-glance checklist against which you can compare the types of facilitation you are already doing or plan to undertake.

It is worth emphasizing here that the facilitation model we are offering provides a means by which you can amend or update your existing style and materials, so don't throw the baby out with the bath water! Many of the things you are already doing could be enhanced and given increased relevance if they are systematically considered in the light of the principles detailed in this chapter.

Planned learning outcomes

By the time you have worked your way through this chapter you should have a clearer understanding of:

- *The importance of a systematic approach.*
- *The Real-world Facilitation leading principle.*
- *Our use of the terms 'relevant', 'significant' and 'meaningful'.*
- *The planning, delivery and future action principles.*
- *The types of questions it might be useful to ask yourself when planning or running a training course.*

THE IMPORTANCE OF A SYSTEMATIC APPROACH

When passengers step off a plane having reached their destination, they are usually unaware of all the careful planning that has gone into every aspect of their flight. Long before the plane even leaves the runway at the point of departure, many hours of preparation, planning, coordination and projection have taken place. For example, the plane will have been checked inside and out, a flight path chosen, passenger list prepared, a flight crew designated, tickets issued. Once in the air, constant checking and re-checking of altitude, course, weather, airspeed and arrival time will have occurred.

As with a successful flight, successful facilitation which produces meaningful learning also requires a careful and systematic approach, in order that each stage of the facilitation process is fully thought through and co-ordinated. That's not to say that you will be able to plan and be ready for every eventuality. Just as the pilot and navigator have to allow for changes in the weather and other unforeseen occurrences, so you too will have to remain flexible, ready and able to deal with occurrences in the learning group which may push you off course, requiring you to make adjustments to your course plan, substituting one exercise or method for another better suited to the situation.

In proposing that you adopt a systematic approach to facilitation we will be using the term 'learning event'. This term describes any significant aspect of a training course which takes learning forward in some way. It might be to do with the learners' awareness of themselves, their awareness of an issue, their ability and preparedness to deal with that issue or perhaps new information on a subject.

Such learning events are subject to an array of different influencing factors, most of which are in the control of the facilitator. These factors include such things as:

- The way the course was planned.
- The chosen (planned) learning outcomes; you might call these aims, goals, objectives or learning intentions.
- The choice of exercises to be used.
- The choice of content, or the areas, issues and problems which will be focused on.
- The structure of the course – the sequence of course elements, how the course is to develop.
- The style, skill, commitment and sensitivity of the facilitators eg, the way they handle and facilitate the group, how conflict, group dynamics and group discomfort are dealt with and so on.
- Ownership of the learning process, and flexibility to allow for this.
- Methods of feedback adopted – how exercises are discussed and made sense of.
- How strategies for dealing with identified problems are developed and by whom.
- Readiness or reluctance to confront or deal with issues raised on the part of the facilitator or the learner.

This is by no means an exhaustive list, and your own experience will suggest many more aspects of the facilitation process which in one way or another influence the type and effectiveness of learning events.

There are many aspects of your facilitation which will directly affect such learning events and these, in turn, influence and combine with each other. For example, your choice of exercises will directly affect the readiness or reluctance of group members to confront and deal with important issues, as will your own chosen facilitation style. (See also Figure 2.1 which outlines the interplay between planning and delivery phases of course design.)

Pause for Thought

- *Try and identify aspects of your own training that have influenced learning events for your learners.*
- *In those circumstances, was your choice of exercise, method, focus, learning outcome, etc. effective and appropriate? Did it encourage learning events? If so, how and why?*
- *Try and add some additional factors to the list above from your own experience.*

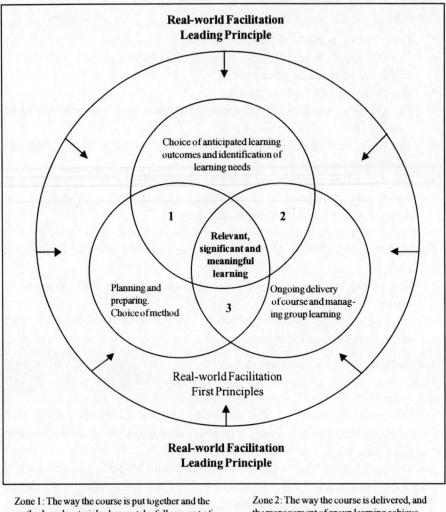

Real-world Facilitation Leading Principle

Choice of anticipated learning outcomes and identification of learning needs

1

2

Relevant, significant and meaningful learning

Planning and preparing. Choice of method

3

Ongoing delivery of course and managing group learning

Real-world Facilitation First Principles

Real-world Facilitation Leading Principle

Zone 1: The way the course is put together and the methods and materials chosen, take full account of anticipated learning outcomes and identified learning needs

Zone 2: The way the course is delivered, and the management of group learning achieve anticipated learning outcomes and meet identified learning needs

Zone 3: The way the course is delivered, whilst retaining flexibility, follows course plan

Figure 2.1 *Both the leading principle and in turn the first principles that flow from it should influence each aspect of the facilitative process in order to maximize relevant, significant and meaningful learning for the learner*

At this point we need to join some arguments together:

- In Chapter 1 we suggested that people learn best when the issues and problems they are working on make sense to them and are relevant to their own everyday experiences; simply put, such issues are live, real and meaningful to them.
- We have also suggested that methods, exercises and materials which encourage and facilitate consideration of such real-world issues at the same time encourage and facilitate effective learning.
- In addition, we have identified the ways in which facilitative choices impact upon such learning events at every stage of the learning process by shaping learning outcomes.

The consequence of these arguments, when taken together, is that effective Real-world Facilitation demands *a systematic approach to the learning process at every stage*, ie, from the point at which you establish the learning needs of the group, through the process of planning a course to the point at which you deliver it and work with the group to achieve anticipated learning outcomes. *At each and every stage of this process, issues of meaning, significance and relevance to the learner must be considered and addressed.*

The best way to develop a systematic approach to your facilitation (and thereby encourage meaningful and relevant learning for your students) is to apply the various Real-world Facilitation principles detailed in this chapter.

To make these principles more accessible we have grouped them under the following headings, each of which relates to a certain part of the facilitative process:

The Leading Principle
Planning Principles
Delivery Principles
Future Action Principles

Pause for Thought

- *As you read through each principle, imagine how it will affect the way you facilitate now.*
- *If you are new to facilitation, reading the principles will provide a good starting point for you. How committed are you to applying them and ensuring that your training courses are immediately relevant and meaningful to the learner?*

THE LEADING PRINCIPLE

This is the over-arching Real-world Facilitation principle from which all other principles are derived.

Learning should be relevant, significant and meaningful to the learner *at every stage* of the facilitative process. It should make sense and be of use in the learner's real world.

Figure 2.1 illustrates how this leading principle, combined with the more specific planning, delivery and future action principles which follow from it, maximizes relevant, significant and meaningful learning when each is applied to your facilitation in a comprehensive and *systematic* way. The diagram also describes how each aspect of planning and delivering a training course should dovetail together if they are to result in a coherent and considered approach to learning.

The leading principle is built around the central themes of *relevant*, *significant* and *meaningful* learning. We see these themes as being so important that it is worth considering each of them in more detail now. A thorough understanding and commitment to their role in the facilitative process is the key to an understanding of what a real-world approach to facilitation is.

Our use of the term 'relevant'

We have ourselves been learners on several courses where other group members came from different occupational backgrounds to our own. While this rich diversity of experience and viewpoint contributed greatly to the over-all learning process, we found that certain exercises and learning sessions we were asked to participate in focused on areas that lacked immediate, direct and obvious relevance to us. The use of psychodrama in group therapy is an example.

On reflection, we found that we gained the best and most long-lasting learning from those parts of such courses which were most clearly and easily transferable to our everyday experiences. These learning phases proved useful to us precisely because they *were* immediately and directly *relevant* to us, keying into our own real-world situations and problems.

As facilitators on a series of in-house training seminars aimed at encouraging employees to embrace a corporate mission statement and its associated values, we were again faced with this same dilemma, in that course participants had been drawn from widely different jobs, functions and roles within the organization. These groups consisted of typists, catering assistants, mechanics, admin. officers and operational police officers. Each learner had a different role, different responsibilities, different backgrounds and came to the training session with different day-to-day experiences, problems and expectations.

It was immediately apparent that relevance was a major issue, as some learners rightly asked questions such as, 'How does this mission statement relate to me and my current role?' Some students, feeling that both the content and design of the course had been designed primarily with operational police staff in mind, said they had found the training day difficult to relate to and largely irrelevant to their current needs.

While factors which influence how *meaningful* learning is are largely *internal* to the learner (eg, attitudes, values, beliefs, ways of understanding and interpreting, existing knowledge, etc.), factors which influence learner *relevance* tend to be those which are *external* to the learner. We have already identified some of these factors by highlighting such things as job, role and function; in addition we might add influences such as education, interests and hobbies, cultural background, religion, etc. Consider Figure 2.2 which offers a graphical interpretation of the influence of internal and external factors on learning.

Clearly you will be unable to address each and every one of these factors when considering the relevance of different aspects of your facilitation, but you can consider the make-up and background of your learners from the start and build strategies into your learning programme which will allow you to take account of such diversity. Further, by considering factors which might affect relevance from an early stage, you will be better able to identify and respond to indications that learners are struggling to relate to what is going on when you actually run the training course.

Later in the book we will be discussing methods of maximizing relevance, even with very diverse groups. For example, we will discuss the use of core learning exercises which provide a basic exercise structure and then encourage participants to generate the content and issues to be worked on for themselves, ensuring that the learning that results is relevant and pertinent to all group members.

Unfortunately, the fact that the learning process is directly relevant to the learner does not in itself guarantee that such learning will be instantly meaningful. Learners encouraged to confront difficult and challenging issues may

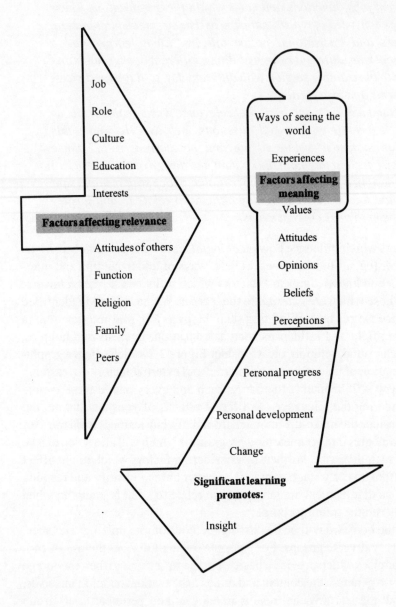

Job

Role

Culture

Education

Interests

Ways of seeing the world

Experiences

Factors affecting meaning

Values

Factors affecting relevance

Attitudes

Attitudes of others

Opinions

Function

Beliefs

Religion

Perceptions

Family

Peers

Personal progress

Personal development

Change

Significant learning promotes:

Insight

Figure 2.2 *External influences and internal factors must all be taken into account to achieve relevant, significant and meaningful learning for the learner*

resist any full understanding of the significance, meaning and consequences of such issues, even though these are obviously relevant to them.

Our use of the term 'significant'

We are using this term to embrace the idea that learning should be of *consequence* to the learner; it should make a difference, allowing him or her to move forward, through personal progress and development, in the area being addressed. For instance, a learner may experience a 'significant emotional event', whereby some long-held belief is challenged and/or changed, or there is a highly charged emotional response to some new learning. Alternatively, the learning may be of intellectual significance in that the assimilation of new information impacts on the way the learner will subsequently view the issue being considered.

> *On a facilitator's course at Surrey University some years ago, led by a facilitator for whom we both have the highest regard, one of us was drawn, through role play, into an emotional realization that the most difficult aspect of breaking the news of a death to a friend or relative, was not so much the act itself (despite its traumatic nature), but coping with the inappropriate humour of colleagues after the event. This was significant learning in that it introduced a new way of looking at and thinking about the issues involved. This was role play based on a real event which encouraged learning that had consequences for the way we thought about and acted in our real world.*

A lack of significance will undoubtedly produce an opposite effect. Learners will not move forward in respect of the topic and may leave feeling they have achieved little more than the chance to restate what they knew or felt at the outset. The planning and delivery of any facilitated course, if it is to maximize meaningful learning, must take full account of the knowledge, skills and views already existent within the group while encouraging learners to build upon and develop these wherever possible.

Our use of the term 'meaningful'

When people enter a learning environment and begin the process of listening, thinking and reflecting, they become engaged in a constant attempt to capture the meaning of what is being said and done. This is an ongoing process in which learners try to link-in any new information or behaviour with the things that they 'know' or understand to be the case already – links with their own experience, knowledge and understanding.

Accordingly, facilitated learning which constantly strives to bridge the divide between theory and practice, classroom and workplace and between new and existing knowledge and experience, greatly assists the learner in this process of establishing these necessary links which ultimately make learning meaningful.

If learners are asked to take part in exercises or activities which bear little or no perceived relation to their lived experience generally, it becomes much more difficult for them to make these necessary links with established knowledge and understanding. The consequence might be that the learner is left searching for meaning.

> *An exercise we have often seen used called 'Star Power' illustrates this point. The exercise itself is intended to explore the issues surrounding class and social differences and the advantages and disadvantages which might attach to different social positions. This is achieved through the use of a simulation game in which learners are divided into groups that trade counters with each other in accordance with fixed rules. In the game, the dice and the rules are loaded in such a way that eventually, as in society generally, a small powerful élite is formed, a group which is given the power to re-write the rules by which the game will be played from that point on.*
>
> *The problems we have observed with this activity arise for two reasons, both of which are pertinent to our consideration of meaningful learning. First, facilitators spend too long running the learning activity itself. They fail to provide the necessary time and opportunity for learners to feed back their own experiences, for them to reflect on and capture the links between the simulated world of the training session and real-world instances of disadvantage and deprivation they may have identified, witnessed or experienced for themselves. Second, during the feedback phase, facilitators consistently fail to assist learners to draw out the real-life meaning of the exercise, focusing instead on what happened within each group during the process of the game itself. For some reason many facilitators seem reluctant to encourage their learners to consider the many parallels that exist between the exercise and real life. This has the effect of restricting learning to a fairly superficial and insignificant (process-oriented) level which*

fails to encourage learners to make sense of what they have experienced in terms of its consequences for future action and attitudes.

In such circumstances it is the very process of seeing the parallels and establishing the links between classroom activity and the world of everyday-life which makes the learning experience meaningful. If the links are not made, such meaning inevitably becomes lost and the relevance and significance of the exercise will rightly be called into question.

Factors which are internal to the learners such as their experiences, attitudes, opinions and beliefs and ways of understanding and interpreting new information will all impact upon new learning (see Figure 2.2). Because learners need to link into these internal factors in order to fully capture the meaning of what they are experiencing, it should be a key aspect of the facilitator's work to encourage them to make these necessary associations and to think about and reflect upon the consequences of such learning for their real world.

PLANNING PRINCIPLES

These principles apply to the planning and preparing stages, such as negotiating and writing learning outcomes, course design, selection of exercises, etc.

- The course aim and accompanying planned learning outcomes (you might call these aims, goals, objectives, or learning intentions) should be relevant, realistic, achievable and applicable to the learner's real world.
- Planned learning outcomes should take account of the learner's self-identified learning needs in addition to any set by their employer or sponsor.
- Exercises and learning activity should be chosen which either use learner experiences and real-world situations as their content or are, alternatively, flexible and transferable exercises which can be used as needed to facilitate issues as they arise.
- The course structure should be sufficiently flexible to allow for group members to set parts of the learning agenda themselves.

DELIVERY PRINCIPLES

These principles apply to facilitation choices at the point of course delivery.

- Your facilitation should draw upon the learner's own experiences, particularly those brought from outside the group, as a central and recurring theme.

- As you facilitate, you should draw upon the everyday situations of the learner, recreating the contexts within which learning will be put into action.
- Confront and deal with actual or potential issues and problems as they do or might arise for the learner within these real-world contexts.
- You should use meaningful everyday language and terms which make sense to the learning group.
- Your facilitative style should take account of and use the learner's existing knowledge and skills in the best possible way.
- When dealing with interpersonal skills, take account of the learner's existing and potential relationships such as:

  - learner and peers
  - learner and subordinates
  - learner and supervisors
  - learner and customer
  - learner and facilitator.

- When you feed exercises back, continually emphasize the need for real-world, workable applications for group and individual learning, strategy forming and commitment to future action.

FUTURE ACTION PRINCIPLES

The future action principles relate to those parts of the course during which learners are encouraged to develop strategies for dealing with their own relevant issues and problems and establish commitment to necessary future action.

- Strategies that you encourage group members to develop in response to their own problems and issues should take account of:

  - the environment in which the strategy will ultimately be used
  - the power, or lack of it, of the learner in any given situation
  - any potential 'costs and benefits' to the learner of the chosen strategy
  - the skills required to put the strategy into practice
  - possible resistance to the strategy which they might discover within themselves or in others.

- Strategies that learners develop in order to deal with their own issues and problems should be realistic and achievable in the real world.

- You should attempt to maximize personal commitment on the part of the learner to put into practice strategies developed on the course.
- In the real world, people need support. Try to generate realistic ideas about how the individual or group might seek out and use the support that is available. ·

This book is intended to be a practical guide for encouraging meaningful learning. What this boils down to is that its contents and ideas are meant to be *used*, becoming translated into action by *you* as you plan, run and evaluate your own training. Nowhere is this more important than here, at the point of departure, because it is only by *systematically* adopting and applying these first principles that you will make certain that learning becomes anchored in terms of real-world meaning and relevance, ensuring that such learning is far more likely to be long-lasting, significant and translated into action and necessary change where it matters.

As we look in more detail at the various aspects of facilitating group learning in the chapters to follow, we will return again and again to these first principles, suggesting how they might be applied in different training situations and with different learning groups. At various points we will also ask you to think through the problems and consequences of applying them in your own facilitation (that is, your real world). By this means we hope to encourage you to draw from your own experience and to utilize your own existing skills and knowledge to test out, and where necessary, amend the ways in which you think about and go about the business of encouraging learning for your students.

CHAPTER 3

Reviewing Current Methods and Materials

Outline

Developing reflective practice is an important part of learning and personal development. This chapter seeks to encourage you to think carefully about your current approach to facilitating learning, by reflecting on how you plan the courses you run, the way in which you work with the group and your choice and use of learning activities and structured exercises. The Real-world Facilitation principles described in the previous chapter are used as benchmarks against which your facilitative style and methods may be compared and contrasted.

Planned learning outcomes

Having worked your way through this chapter we hope you will have a better understanding of:

- *The ways in which all aspects of your training work together to influence learning outcomes.*
- *Your current approach to planning and preparing facilitated training courses and its compatibility with Real-world Facilitation principles.*

- *The way you work with the learning group at the point of training delivery and its effectiveness in maximizing relevant, significant and meaningful learning for your group.*
- *Your choice and use of learning activities and exercises and how they impact on the overall success or failure of a training course in real-world terms.*

A REALISTIC AND WORKABLE APPROACH

One important aspect of Real-world Facilitation is its emphasis on the need to both recognize and utilize the existing knowledge, skills and experiences that learners bring with them into any training setting. What takes place within the learning environment will be understandable to the learner largely in terms of what he or she knows and has already experienced. New information and new ways of looking at things must first be grasped by relating them to a previously learned background of information, ideas and attitudes. Real-world Facilitation strives to maximize this assimilation process by bridging the new and the known, clarifying and shaping new ideas by linking them with the learner's existing experiences and knowledge.

As a reader of this book you have many things in common with a learner on a training course. Accordingly, we must acknowledge from the outset that your understanding of and commitment toward the Real-world Facilitation model will be shaped by your existing knowledge and experience of teaching. If you are an experienced facilitator, this will of course include your current methods and materials.

Certainly it would be wise to consider any new approach to facilitation with cautious optimism, keeping one eye on the possible benefits and the other on the costs of adopting new ideas, particularly when this could mean a lot of additional work collecting and designing new learning materials and exercises. Your real world, like ours, probably involves hectic schedules, deadlines and unexpected eventualities, seldom offering much time for planning and preparation.

Acknowledging such constraints and pressures dictates that any strategy we offer you for adopting Real-world Facilitation as a new way of working with your learners must be realistic, achievable and workable if it is to be of any real use. There would be little point in arguing that you should ditch everything you are currently doing in favour of the new ideas and practices contained in this book. Such an approach would fail to realise and maximize aspects of your existing facilitation which work for you, nor would it be a workable and realistic strategy in your real world.

Pause for Thought

Think back to the last training session you facilitated and identify:

- *Things you did that promoted real-world learning.*
- *Things you might have done or changed which would have encouraged real-world learning.*

THE LITMUS TEST

To help clarify the two main methods by which you can measure the compatibility between this real-world approach to facilitation and your own current facilitative methods and materials it could be useful to think about another well-known 'two-tier' measure, the litmus test.

Used to measure the acidity or alkalinity of a substance, the litmus test uses strips of paper coated in a preparation which reacts to levels of acidity by changing colour. If you wanted a rough rule-of-thumb measurement, you could simply dip your litmus paper in the solution and then gauge roughly 'by eye' how much the colour changed. For a more accurate measurement however, you would have to compare the result with various pre-defined shades on the control card, matching the colour more precisely.

In a similar fashion, you could form a general idea of how likely it is that a specific method or exercise will promote and encourage meaningful, relevant and significant learning, by reviewing it in light of the Real-world Facilitation leading principle. This will help you to gain a fair idea as to whether the approach is along the right lines or needs rethinking.

To measure effectiveness (in real-world terms) more closely, it is more useful to compare the aim, intentions, planned use and likely outcomes of any facilitative approach with the *specific* planning, delivery and future action principles of the Real-world Facilitation model. These are our control cards; ie, benchmarks, against which aspects of facilitation can be matched or contrasted, whether they be ways of working with the group, aspects of planning, exercises or any other part of the facilitative process.

When thinking about your current approach in light of the Real-world

Facilitation leading principle and, more specifically, the planning, delivery and future action principles, it is useful to separate out various aspects of facilitation activity into the following four broad categories (see Figure 3.1):

- Your approach to planning and preparation.
- How you work with the learning group.
- Your current choice and use of learning activities.
- Your current choice and use of exercises.

YOUR CURRENT APPROACH TO PLANNING AND PREPARING

Pause for Thought

- *When you are planning and preparing for a new training course, what factors influence your plan? (You may like to jot these down.)*
- *How often do you take account of, and plan to utilize, your learners' existing knowledge, skills and experiences?*
- *How much flexibility do you allow for your learners to build-in their own agenda?*

To some extent, it is a mistaken assumption that good facilitation is all about your performance when working with learners at the point of training delivery. Often, the actual shape and success of a course, indeed the very context within which learning takes place, is largely defined by the course plan, designed in advanced although seldom negotiated with learners beforehand. There are some unfortunate exceptions to this:

- Courses run for which no previous planning has taken place. This can result in a lack of any clear direction for both the facilitator and his or her students. Exercises and learning activities are pulled from the trainer's hat and used without thought as to their relevance and suitability to learner's needs.
- Courses on which the plan is thrown away. In our experience this is often the consequence of a lack of fit between the facilitator's anticipation of what the learners' needs are, and their actual learning needs which become revealed as the course gets under way.
- Learner resistance to the learning plan. This can arise when group members find learning activity and exercises irrelevant, insignificant and lacking in meaning.

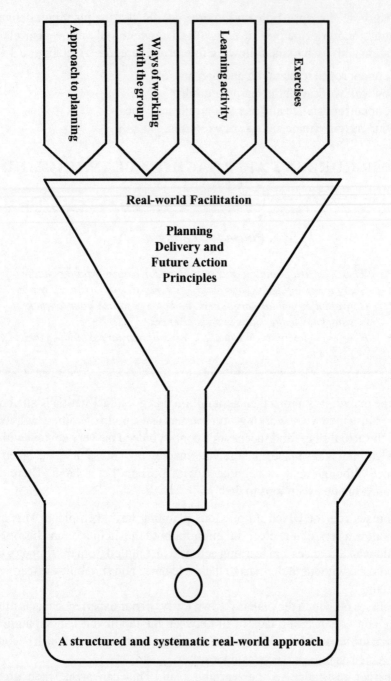

Figure 3.1 *Every part of the process needs to be filtered through the principles of Real-world Facilitation*

Hints on reviewing your current approach to planning

To assist you to review your current approach to planning and preparing, we have included a number of points to consider and questions to answer. As you work through them, be as honest as you can with yourself; after all, no one is looking and you're not being asked to account for the strengths and weaknesses of your current style (see Figure 3.2).

	Approach to planning	Ways of working with the group	Choice and use of learning activity	Choice and use of exercises
Level 1	Fully compatible with Real- world Facilitation leading principle, and appropriate planning, delivery and future action principles. No modification necessary.			
Level 2	Needs certain modifications in the light of Real-world Facilitation leading principle, and appropriate planning, delivery and future action principles.			
Level 3			Learning activity or exercise under review, not real-world, and not susceptible to modification, but are used as they are and legitimized through Real-world feedback.	
Level 4	Not suitable for amendment or modification. Identified as not suitable for encouraging real-world learning.			

Figure 3.2 *Levels of compatibility of existing methods and materials with Real-world principles*

- Imagine what each learning phase will look like, by thinking it through in terms of whether:

  - it is meaningful to the learner, allowing him or her to link new learning to their existing ways of thinking and understanding
  - it is relevant to the learner's needs and experiences allowing for the disclosure of real-world issues, problems and experiences
  - it takes the learner forward, allowing for personal development in the area being addressed
  - you have allowed sufficient time
  - you have accounted for learners' likely span of attention
  - this learning phase builds upon and develops the last phase
  - it will be developed in the next phase.

- Do you provide sufficient flexibility for your learners to build-in their own learning agenda, in respect of each major component of the course?
- Do you plan in terms of learning phases rather than in terms of the use of specific facilitation tools? For example – plan for an issues identification phase which aims to allow learners time to clarify and describe relevant problems, issues and experiences. You can then have ready an array of suitable exercises and learning activities (which focus on issues identification) from which to choose.
- Do you take account of existing skills and knowledge levels in the group, ensuring that learners are not tasked to undertake activity which does not take their learning forward?

REVIEWING HOW YOU WORK WITH LEARNING GROUPS

At the beginning of Chapter 2, we stressed the importance of adopting a systematic approach to your facilitation, arguing that many different ingredients of a training course work together to influence the learning that takes place. For example, the way the course is planned will affect which exercises are used and these aspects will in turn influence the learning that results.

Some particular aspects of facilitation mentioned, amongst the many influencing factors we listed, were the style, skill, commitment and sensitivity of the facilitator, eg, the way he or she handles and facilitates the group, how conflict, group dynamics and group discomfort are handled and resolved.

A full commitment to maximizing effective learning, through the adoption of a real-world approach to facilitation, requires that you think through the way you work with people in learning groups in light of the specific delivery and future action principles detailed in Chapter 2.

Pause for Thought

(Suggestion: As you work through this 'pause for thought' section, why not score yourself out of 10 for each part, eg, if you think that you usually do use everyday language which learners can readily relate to, but that there are times when you use facilitator phrases or other less meaningful terms, you might score yourself a 6 or 7. As there are 10 aspects to be considered, you will easily be able to work out a percentage score.)

* *Think back to a facilitated training session that is typical of those you undertake. When working with the learning group to what extent did you:*

  – *Use meaningful everyday language and terms?*   *(Score /10)*
  – *Draw upon the learner's own experiences as examples?*
            (Score /10)
  – *Work through issues in terms of how they relate to the learner's everyday situations?*   *(Score /10)*
  – *Confront and deal with learner's issues and problems in terms of how they can and do arise in the real world?*   *(Score /10)*
  – *Consider the impact on learning of the student's existing and potential relationships with:*
    Peers?
    Subordinates?
    Managers?
    Supervisors?
    Customers?   *(Score /10 for each)*
  – *Emphasize that learning should be of use in and make a difference to everyday problems, issues and experiences?*
            (Score /10)

         (Total Score = /100)

Your total score should give you some idea of how 'real world' your facilitation is. If you scored, say, less than 50 per cent then you have a fair amount of work to do to make your facilitation relevant, significant and meaningful.

Meaningful language

The use of language is pivotal to the image of the training course as perceived by your learners and is obviously the vehicle through which ideas and information are exchanged and discussed. Accordingly, you should remain constantly aware of the level and style of the language you are using. Is it conveying the right message? Is it clear and unambiguous? Can your learners understand what you are saying? Does your choice and use of language and terms facilitate and encourage learning?

> *As learners we often attend training courses which aim to offer experienced facilitators the opportunity to develop their skills. We can usually predict that on such courses there will be continual use of stock facilitator phrases such as, 'Take that on board' or 'Thank you for sharing that', etc.*
> *The danger of such language is that it is seldom used in everyday conversation, and can often sound insincere or unnecessarily trite and false, thus becoming a barrier to learning. In our experience, it can have the damaging effect of actually undermining learners' faith in both the training and the trainer.*

We would suggest that you should, wherever possible:

- Use everyday terms and language.
- Avoid buzz phrases unless they are currency and thus relevant and meaningful to the learning group.
- Use a learner's own terms if this will assist their understanding or involvement and participation.
- Be aware of your own language and terms and that of others.
- Ask for clarification from learners when they don't make themselves clearly understood by you or other members of the learning group.
- Be sensitive to the use of racist, sexist or other prejudicial conversation or language, particularly your own!
- Avoid swearing; whilst you might reasonably think that this will bolster your credibility by showing that you are in touch with the street culture, you cannot assume that some people in the group will not be offended.

Drawing on learners' experiences as examples

It is extremely helpful to learners when aspects of training are strengthened through illustrative examples. Further, such examples serve a dual purpose in terms of Real-world Facilitation – not only illuminating part of the course, but at the same time placing learning into context by setting it within an everyday framework. Let's provide you with an example.

A trainer on a staff development course disclosed to the group that he found 'rescuing' to be quite difficult behaviour to cope with. He was asked to give a real example of what he meant and he described a situation to the group where a person on a course he was facilitating always jumped in to rescue another learner whenever this second person said something or was asked a question. He went on to describe the destructive effect such rescuing behaviour had on the group dynamic.

By asking for a real world example, the facilitator was able to draw upon the learner's own experiences to both clarify an important issue and to place this in the context of a live training session where its meaning and relevance were greatest.

Opportunities should be taken wherever possible to illustrate and contextualize learner issues and to set possible strategies and solutions against such real-world examples, tasking learners to reflect on whether they are workable, realistic and achievable in such circumstances *from the learner's point of view.*

Relating issues to real-world situations

Pause for Thought

- *When you are working with a learning group, and live issues or problems are unearthed that need confronting, how do you facilitate this?*
- *What questions would you ask, or encourage learners to ask themselves, in order to relate such issues to the real-world contexts within which they must be confronted and addressed?*

In Figure 3.3 we have provided some suggested questions which will encourage and enable learners to:

- Clarify the nature of the issue or problem being focused upon.
- Identify how and when such issues and problems can and do arise and what can happen when they do.
- Think about and formulate real-world strategies and solutions to these

identified issues and problems which are achievable and realistic in a real-world setting.

Confronting issues by placing them in a real-world context

On a training course on equal opportunities that we ran, we established, through an issues-identification phase, that attitudes towards gypsy travellers were important to the group.

Having reached this level of disclosure we then worked with the group to clarify existing and potential problems that certain attitudes and prejudices could provoke, encouraging group members to explore the likely real-world consequences of both thinking and dealing with travellers as 'lawbreakers' and 'second-class citizens'.

Taking the group beyond disclosure in this way was helpful, in that it facilitated their consideration of instances of such prejudice in the real world and of its likely results for all concerned.

The impact of relationships

One significant feature of group work, which it shares with the learners' day-to-day experiences outside the training setting, is that the learning which occurs is influenced by both existing and new relationships which form as the course unfolds.

Interpersonal relationships can have a large impact on learning and must be acknowledged and accounted for. How realistic is it, for example, to encourage learners to identify relevant issues, problems and experiences from their own real world, if such disclosure points towards a difficult relationship between workers, or between a worker and a supervisor, when both of them are present in the group? Such an occurrence is highly likely and could undoubtedly prove very useful in the promotion of real-world learning. But, it *must* be carefully facilitated so as to allow open and honest reflection and agreement concerning realistic and workable solutions.

A real-world issue identified by a learner on a team-building course initially appeared to arise from his own confusion over the exact nature and extent of his supervisory role in the company.

His supervisor was also a learner on the course, and his reaction to this disclosure suggested discomfort and unease. We noted this, and encouraged the supervisor to tell the group his thoughts on the issue raised.

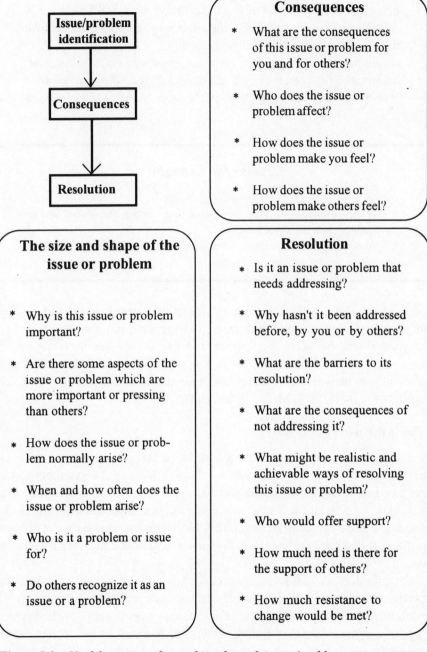

Issue/problem identification

↓

Consequences

↓

Resolution

Consequences

* What are the consequences of this issue or problem for you and for others?

* Who does the issue or problem affect?

* How does the issue or problem make you feel?

* How does the issue or problem make others feel?

The size and shape of the issue or problem

* Why is this issue or problem important?

* Are there some aspects of the issue or problem which are more important or pressing than others?

* How does the issue or problem normally arise?

* When and how often does the issue or problem arise?

* Who is it a problem or issue for?

* Do others recognize it as an issue or a problem?

Resolution

* Is it an issue or problem that needs addressing?

* Why hasn't it been addressed before, by you or by others?

* What are the barriers to its resolution?

* What are the consequences of not addressing it?

* What might be realistic and achievable ways of resolving this issue or problem?

* Who would offer support?

* How much need is there for the support of others?

* How much resistance to change would be met?

Figure 3.3 *Useful questions for working through issues/problems, consequences and resolutions*

He went on to admit that perhaps his colleague's problem was actually his fault in that he often did things himself which were in fact the direct responsibility of the other person, and he had become aware of the frustration this was causing.

A solution was agreed which involved a commitment to better communication between them, and an undertaking by the supervisor to invest a greater degree of trust in the other's ability to get the job done.

Pause for Thought

- *What relationships can you identify as being influential in the training you facilitate?*
- *In what ways have you acknowledged and accounted for such relationships in your facilitation?*

Such relationships will often exist outside of the immediate training setting, but must be acknowledged and accounted for none the less. Relationships between peers, between the learner and his or her senior managers or supervisor and the learner and his or her subordinates, together with those relationships between the learner and the customer, can all be significant aspects of real-world problems, issues and experiences.

What's the use of learning?

A criticism we often overhear being levelled at facilitated training courses is that they are nothing more than talking shops, a form of elongated unproductive meeting, where lots of discussion takes place but nothing worthwhile ever gets done. As a trainer it is easy to become defensive about such attitudes by blaming learner cynicism or negativity. None the less, this does not account for the fact that such feelings, whether justly held or not, are very real for the person expressing them.

The adoption of a real-world approach, realized through careful review and revision of your existing facilitative methods and materials, together with a commitment to the Real-world Facilitation model itself, will become translated into a way of thinking about and working with learners which *systematically and at every stage maximizes the usefulness and relevance of learning for them.*

Learners will see the sense and usefulness of training which requires them to constantly draw upon and use their own ways of viewing and understanding the topic and their own experiences, knowledge and skills. They will value an approach which asks them to identify their own live issues and problems in the area being discussed, and which works with them to confront such issues, beginning to address and resolve them through the formulation of realistic and workable strategies.

This will require a selective approach to facilitating learning which continually strives to raise and explore real-world issues and real everyday contexts. Learners do not always make this an easy task and some, inevitably, will stray from the point or shoot off at a tangent at the very moment when you feel the group is starting to hit a useful and rewarding seam. Part of your skill will be in deciding the degree of refocusing required and how this is best achieved.

It should also be emphasized here that far from dismissing or rejecting theory input, a real-world approach complements and clarifies that input. What better way could there be of making theoretical arguments relevant and meaningful, than to encourage learners to test their validity and application in the real world of everyday life? How does the theory translate in real terms? Does it fit with the learners' own experiences? Are its explanations meaningful and useful? Does the model capture and explain aspects of the world of everyday life?

Pause for Thought

- *Think about any theoretical input you give to your learners, in light of this section. Can you identify ways of enhancing its relevance, significance and meaning that fit with your facilitative style?*

EXERCISES AND LEARNING ACTIVITY

Figure 3.4 provides a graphical illustration of the important differences between what we have termed 'learning activity' and 'exercises'. Such separation serves not only to clarify our use of these terms, but can also be useful to you when reviewing and revising your own methods and materials.

The more responsive and spontaneous nature of learning activities makes them ideal tools for capturing and using ideas as they are raised by your learners, for focusing or refocusing the group and for generating issues, problems experiences and solutions.

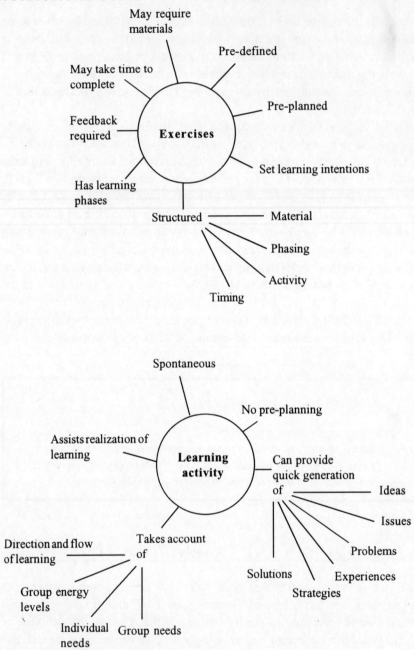

Figure 3.4 *Main characteristics of exercises and learning activities*

Examples of learning activity include:

- Spontaneous brainstorming.
- Unplanned small-group discussion.
- On-the-spot role play.
- Quick input by the facilitator (explaining a model that illustrates the issues being discussed, for example).
- A 'Round-Robin' type activity where, for example, each group member in turn is asked to give a brief reaction or idea concerning the issue being discussed.
- Defining terms with which the group might be having difficulty.
- Ranking unexpected responses to clarify their importance to the group.

Exercises differ from learning activities in that they tend to be planned and structured, often with a pre-set aim and corresponding learning intentions. Following involvement in such exercises, learners are normally encouraged to continue around the learning cycle by reflecting on the experience in terms of consequences and usefulness. Examples of exercises include:

- Pre-planned role play.
- Structured simulation of a real-world event.
- Case-studies.
- Structured problem-solving.
- Published 'off-the-peg' exercises.

Earlier in this chapter we provided a table (Figure 3.2) which outlined four basic levels of compatibility between the methods and materials you are currently using and the Real-world Facilitation model. As you work through the process of review and reflection it is probable that you will find some aspects of your approach more 'in tune' than others with this new approach; indeed, one purpose of discussing levels of compatibility is to encourage you to think about modification rather than rejection where this is possible, perhaps changing the way you work with your material as well as changing the material itself.

- Full compatibility with the Real-world Facilitation leading principle and appropriate planning, delivery and future action principles.

Here, your exercises and learning activity systematically draw on the learner's knowledge, skills and experience while encouraging the identification of relevant real-world problems and issues. Your choice and use of exercises and learning activities encourages learners to address these concerns by reflecting on their real-world consequences and implications, before thinking out realistic and achievable ways of dealing with them in everyday contexts such as in the workplace.

The most effective way of maximizing the relevance and significance of learning realized through learning activities and exercises is to make them what we would term *core exercises* and *core learning activities*. By this we mean a style of activity which provides learners with a loose framework or skeleton within which they can use their own issues, problems and experiences as the content to be worked through.

An example of this approach would be where the facilitator has pre-planned a role-play exercise, but has left the actual details of the scenario to be generated by the learners. Alternatively, the facilitator may decide to move into a learning phase where learners move into a small group to discuss an issue that has arisen. Although it is the facilitator who has decided in which way the learning process will proceed, ideally the content of that unplanned discussion will have been suggested by contributions made by members of the group.

- Material may need certain changes in light of both the Real-world Facilitation leading principle and specific planning, delivery and future action principles.

Much of your existing material may require only slight modifications rather than a complete overhaul. Be economical initially by identifying the aspects of your existing exercises and learning activities which work well and already promote forms of real-world learning.

Keep a copy of the original so that, should your modified approach not work as well as you had hoped, you can return to the original and consider both old and revised versions in terms of your experiences of each.

Think about any changes you propose to make in terms of:

- How they will actually work in practice. Imagine yourself facilitating the modified activity or exercise in a training setting. Are the changes sufficient to ensure the encouragement of real-world learning; conversely, are they too drastic?
- What it would be like to undertake the activity or exercise. Imagine it from a learner's point of view: does it allow learners to bring in their own issues, problems and experiences?
- How do any changes you make to an activity or exercise impact upon its stated aim and planned learning outcomes? These may need to be changed in light of modifications.
- Having made necessary modifications or changes to an exercise or learning activity consider it once again in terms of the specific real-world principles detailed in Chapter 2.

- Not a real-world exercise or learning activity but linkable through feed-back.

Having reviewed certain exercises it may be that some do not easily lend themselves to modification in the way we have described. This can often be the case with the larger simulation-type exercises which encourage awareness-raising or confronting of issues through learner involvement in role-playing scenarios designed to simulate aspects of the real world.

An example of this form of exercise is a simulation called 'cultures'. In the first part of this large exercise, learners are split into four groups, each being assigned a culture to work on; agricultural, industrial, revolutionary and technological. Each group then takes on one of the cultures as its own, agreeing its norms, values, traditions and practices, these decisions being made through group agreement and collective response to a series of prompt cards such as 'marriage arrangements', 'religion', laws and rules' and 'type of dress', etc. In effect, students build the framework of the culture by sharing their collective ideas on what its shape and nature should be.
In the second part of the exercise, a member of each group is forced to emigrate to another, previously unknown, culture, the members of which subject him or her to a compatibility interview before deciding on entry requirements and conditions.

Here the exercise provides each learner with the issues to be discussed and addressed, the problems to be solved and the means by which each of these things might be achieved. The actual task of constructing a culture from the ground up does not attempt to draw upon and utilize learners' lived experience in any direct way. Likewise the immigration/emigration phase may or may not appear relevant and meaningful to those involved at the time.

However, in the very act of playing out the prescribed scenario with its attached roles, an experience is created to which learners undoubtedly bring their everyday values, attitudes and opinions. These ways of looking at and thinking about people and situations are fundamental to an understanding of real-world issues, problems and experiences. What is needed in order to maximize this real-world learning potential in such circumstances is careful, considered and facilitated feedback which encourages students to systemati-cally draw this learning out of the training experience and translate and link it into typical everyday situations where ways of thinking about and behaving towards others do have real and important consequences and outcomes.

This task of careful and considered feedback can be easier if you approach it with some sort of structure. The questions provided in Figure 3.3 may provide some help in this regard and could be used to complement a learning cycle such as that expounded by David Kolb (1975).

• Not suitable for modification or linking through feedback.

You will find, as we have, that certain aspects of your facilitation do not lend themselves to re-working, and accordingly must be considered unsuitable for the purpose of encouraging real-world learning. While it can sometimes be difficult to discard well-used methods and materials, it is important to question their usefulness from the learner's point of view. In a similar way to pruning in the garden, careful and selective pruning of your exercises and learning activities will ensure a stronger, more effective approach which yields purposeful and usable learning.

SUMMARY

Each and every stage of the facilitative process has a significant impact on learning, from the very point of inception, through the initial planning and preparation phases to the actual point of delivery when you are working with the group in the training setting, encouraging learning and commitment to future action and necessary change. Because of the integrated and inter-dependent nature of planning and delivery there is a corresponding need to review and revise your facilitation in a systematic way.

In this chapter we have encouraged you to acknowledge and account for this important fact by providing you with a framework within which to reflect, review and revise your current methods and materials in a systematic and methodical manner, by comparing and contrasting them with the Real-world Facilitation principles.

But an awareness of your current approach and its effectiveness in encouraging and promoting learning which is of use in the learner's real world is only part of the process, for, as with Real-world Facilitation generally, learning should prove its usefulness through translation into necessary action and change. In real terms this requires that you commit yourself to making the modifications and changes to your work that you have identified as being necessary.

This commitment need not, and indeed should not, be too much of a burden on you. Remember, strategies to effect necessary change should be realistic and achievable in *your* real world. It is far better to review and amend your approach as an ongoing project which leads to a gradual and smooth adoption of the Real-world Facilitation model; that way you will be able to practise this new approach and monitor its effects on learning.

CHAPTER 4

Planning and Preparation

Outline

Planning and preparation are vital phases of any facilitated training course and in this chapter we look at both, from the standpoint of Real-world Facilitation. Decisions made at this stage often create the very context within which the course will be placed and learning generated. This point leads us into a discussion of such issues as the construction of aims and planned learning outcomes, flexibility and acknowledgment of the impact of certain environmental features.

Planned learning outcomes

By the time you have finished reading this chapter we anticipate that:

- *You will be more aware of the ways in which planning and preparation influence and shape eventual learning.*
- *You will have considered many of the main issues surrounding the planning and preparation of a facilitated training course.*
- *You will have reviewed the Real-world Facilitation planning principles, thinking through their implications for your training.*
- *You will be better able to frame planned learning outcomes in real-world terms.*
- *You will have thought through issues of learner autonomy.*

REAL WORLD FACILITATION PLANNING PRINCIPLES

Before taking a detailed look at the various issues surrounding planning and preparation, it is important that we first review the specific *planning principles* introduced in Chapter 2. These principles apply to the planning and preparation stages, such as negotiating and writing planned learning outcomes, course design, selection of exercises, etc.

- The course aim and accompanying planned learning outcomes (you might call these objectives or learning intentions) should be relevant, realistic, achievable and applicable to the learner's real world.
- Planned learning outcomes should take account of the learner's self-identified learning needs in addition to any set by their employer or sponsor.
- Exercises and learning activity should be chosen which either use learner experiences and everyday situations as their content, or alternatively, are flexible and transferable exercises which can be used as needed to facilitate issues as they arise.
- The course structure should be sufficiently flexible to allow for group members to set parts of the learning agenda themselves.

PLANNING AND THE CONTEXT OF LEARNING

It cannot be over-emphasized that the planning and preparation phases of any facilitated training course are vitally important. If you have been involved in training for any length of time, this may seem to be like a well-worn message that predicts failure for those who don't follow the 'respected way of doing things'. In truth however, the demands for systematic and thoughtful planning and preparation are based on sound arguments. Yes of course, it is possible that you might get away with planning your next session on the escalator on the way to the course-room, but getting away with it is about the best you can hope for with this approach. If your training stands any chance of being *responsive* to the learning needs of both the organization *and* the learner you will have to invest both time and effort in discovering the nature and extent of such needs, and to consider how you might effectively meet them within the training environment.

Real-world Facilitation places additional demands on you in this regard, requiring that you also think carefully about meeting specified learning needs within a real-world framework, in order to ensure that resultant learning is useful, makes sense, can be related to everyday situations, and can meet and resolve real-world problems and issues.

Although it may sound something of a contradiction in terms, Real-world Facilitation additionally requires that you design flexibility into your training plan, allowing space for learners to raise and set their own course agenda, an agenda which contains *their* real-world issues, problems and concerns, problems that are live and pressing for them, in terms of the topic being discussed.

When taken together, these requirements suggest that there are many fundamental decisions to be made when planning any facilitated training course; decisions that will heavily influence learning by creating the very context within which that training will take place and find meaning. We want that context to be a *real-world* one, in which the motivation to learn, and the level and significance of the contributions and disclosures that underpin that learning, are directed towards the development of useable skills, and the formulation of workable and realistic solutions and strategies that have practical applications. In this way your learners will become better equipped to address and resolve the ongoing issues, problems and experiences that form part of their everyday lives.

To better understand the nature of these fundamental planning decisions, and their impact upon resultant learning, it would be useful to consider them in summary.

- The aim and planned learning outcomes of the course.

The overall course aim and its associated planned learning outcomes will frame your decision-making during the planning phase, and will become a form of criteria against which both you and the learning group will measure learning outcomes. At this point in the argument it is important to stress five points in relation to the formulation of both the course aim and planned learning outcomes (both of which will be considered in greater detail within later sections):

- Each planned learning outcome should be designed from a real-world standpoint, conforming to the requirements of the relevant planning principles, by seeking to account for, and work with, issues and problems which are relevant and significant to course members.
- The planned learning outcomes you design should be structured so as to openly encourage the transfer and application of learning to real-world situations.
- The number and scope of planned learning outcomes should be realistic

and achievable, allowing each major aspect of the course to be dealt with in sufficient and appropriate depth.
- A planned learning outcome should be included that specifically addresses the identification and consideration of barriers to the transfer of learning to real-world situations.
- The course aim and planned learning outcomes should, as far as possible, reflect the stated needs of both the sponsor and the course members.

• The shape of the course (its structure).

Decisions relating to course structure should include consideration of such matters as timing and emphasis. You will have to decide how the time you have available should be divided into the various learning phases. This decision will also have an impact upon the amount of emphasis you feel a particular phase, exercise, or activity deserves when compared to other parts of the course. The structure of any course is also closely connected with its development.

• How your course will unfold (its development).

By allowing for the logical development of learning phases, you will help your learners in their ongoing task of drawing meaning and relevance from their experiences in the training setting. Each phase can be thought of as a building block which, while building on those blocks previously placed in position, serves to support the learning blocks that follow. Much of what we have said about encouraging real-world learning rests upon this building process. For example, we have argued that there is a need to move from any initial phase (during which real-world problems and issues become exposed and identified), to a phase in which exercises and learning activity seek to focus on the impact and everyday consequences of such issues and problems for the learner. Having considered such consequences and implications, the group would then expect to progress to the next stages of learning, in which the training encourages and enables learners to formulate, discuss and validate strategies and solutions in response to such issues and problems. Such a developmental path through these various learning phases provides a coherent and structured sequencing of the learning programme, that fits naturally with the existing sequences of problem-solving used on a day-to-day basis by most learners: that is, identification/clarification, consideration/implication and application/resolution.

Due account must also be taken of each learner's need to become part of the learning group and for their need to adjust to the demands of the learning environment (which may well stand in contrast to their normal day-to-day experiences). Brundage and Mackeracher (1980) suggest that:

63

adults, when they enter a new learning experience, begin with dependent-type behaviour and move first to independent behaviour and then to interdependent behaviour during the course of learning activity (pp.54–55).

This model of progression is useful in highlighting the need for planning which allows both time and space for learners to make necessary personal adjustments and transitions, providing room for the learner to 'grow into' an effective learning relationship with the larger group, a relationship that is characterized by integration and interdependence.

- What exercises and learning activity are appropriate?

Closely linked with issues of structure and development are the planning decisions you make concerning which learning exercises and activities are to be used to facilitate the learning you hope to promote. Unless they are what we have termed *'core exercises'*, or *'core learning activities'* (see Chapter 3 for a detailed account of these types of exercise and learning activity), it is likely that your choice of facilitative exercise or learning activity will tend to steer people's learning in a particular direction. This is because the content of these pre-structured exercises and learning activities (and the way that learners both work with and react to them) pre-suppose certain learning conclusions which are inherent within their layout and design. Unfortunately, the direction dictated may not be the one in which learners either want or expect their learning to proceed. Accordingly, it is vital that you consider how these exercises influence course development, as, by imposing certain choices upon your learners, you could easily impose particular direction on their learning.

- How flexible will the course be?

All too often, decisions made during planning fail to account for the need to design in flexibility. A tight and unyielding training plan, built on presumptions of what learners need, cannot provide sufficient opportunity for the learning group to build its own learning agenda *together*, in terms of the subject area being dealt with on the course. Even where facilitators have had the benefit of pre-course tutorials with individual learners, and have worked with them to identify areas of significance and need, due account must be taken of the extra dimension arising from group interaction during any agenda-building phase. This demands flexibility in terms of course structure, development and the choice and use of training exercises and activities. In short, the group, as a learning unit, needs the facility of a responsive and dynamic training plan, which allows for a balance between pre-set (often organizational goals and planned learning outcomes) and learner-generated agendas that reflect real-world issues, problems experiences and concerns.

> No learner can be effective in more than a very limited area if he or she cannot make decisions for themselves about what they should be learning and how they should be learning it ... If students are denied [these] opportunities to participate in decision making about their learning, they are less likely to develop the skills they need in order to plan and organise for life-long learning (Boud, 1988, pp.17 and 22).

- How much space will there be for learners to set and work through their own agenda?

This may seem to be a duplicate decision to that concerning flexibility in course design that we discussed above, but this is not the case. Any initial decisions concerning the need to design in flexibility to allow for the building of a group course agenda must also become linked with (and will be complemented by) further decisions concerning the way in which this group agenda is to be balanced with the ongoing requirement to address specific learning needs, as these are revealed by individual learners as the course develops. It must be emphasized that Real-world Facilitation does not (and must not be allowed to) equate to a form of totally needs-led training, in which learners are allowed to 'chase the tail' of any theme they find of interest. Facilitated learning should be structured, taking place within a responsive, dynamic and flexible training framework, the contours of which are defined by the training plan, course aim and accompanying planned learning outcomes. This, in turn, should promote a learning environment that systematically draws upon and uses real-world issues and experiences as the contextual framework within which the topic is discussed and useful and transferable learning is encouraged.

- Your learners, their expectations and learning needs.

If you want to provide a learning experience for your group that links in directly with their own existing experiences, is anchored in their reality, and which seeks to identify and deal with their significant and pressing problems and concerns, it follows that you will need information about their backgrounds, expectations and learning needs. Ideally, this information should be obtained *before* you begin any systematic planning and preparation, so as to ensure that your planning choices are responsive to the problems, issues and experiences that are important to your learners within the topic area to be

65

addressed. This aspect of planning is dealt with in greater detail in a later section.

- How much account will be taken of learners' existing skills, knowledge and experience?

Part of the richness of the real-world approach to facilitating learning arises from its insistence on both recognizing and maximizing the most valuable resource at any facilitator's disposal: the existing skills, knowledge and experience of the learners themselves. The desire to draw upon and use this resource should permeate each aspect of your facilitative approach, becoming a cherished educational value that is so much a part of your thinking and action as to become virtually inherent. This will take time and commitment, and we would recommend that during your early attempts to systematically account for and make use of your learners' existing knowledge, skills and experiences, you should make a conscious decision to 'design in' opportunities where this can occur. Keep in mind how much of the learning agenda is being pre-set, either by the constraints of the syllabus you must work to, or by your interpretation and application of it. Even where there is not much opportunity for learner autonomy in agenda-setting, there is no reason why you should not systematically attempt to relate prescribed sections of the course to the day-to-day experiences of your learners.

Remember also that significant learning requires that learners move beyond what they already know into areas in which personal development is both possible and desirable. Unless you account for existing levels of knowledge, skill and expertise (taking steps to discover these where they are not known), then learning may be pitched at too low a level, and will fail to stretch and challenge learners.

- Which issues will be addressed and which will not?

In the real world, tough choices often have to be made. Similarly, in the world of facilitation, one of the most difficult choices faced by any facilitator is that posed by the necessity to select those parts of any particular topic which should be focused upon, as distinct from those which should be sacrificed at the altar of time management and realism. A two-day course on interpersonal skills or assertiveness cannot realistically aim to cover the entire spectrum of issues in such vast and ill-defined areas, and must instead extract a small number of themes which can be covered at an appropriate level if learning is to be effective and significant. Later in this chapter we will discuss ways in which questions concerning correct and appropriate focus can be addressed from a real-world standpoint, allowing for due attention to be given to both the nature of the problem (where one exists or is perceived to exist), and the nature of people's learning needs.

- Decisions concerning the learning environment.

Taking account of the learning environment is increasingly becoming a study in its own right. It is an important part of the planning process, and to a certain degree has a dynamic quality in that it impacts upon learning as the course develops.

Analysis of the learning environment has been expounded by Tessmer and Harris (1992). It is surprising, however, that all too often this important aspect of the planning process is given scant attention. This reluctance to plan adequately for the learning environment can have many causes: when there is already so much to think about, having additionally to consider the environment within which learning will take place can prove onerous indeed. Sometimes, a sense of resignation develops, stemming from the view that of all the things we cannot change, resources are surely the most immutable. In the real world, we recognize that you cannot get additional course-room space or furnishings easily, but, as you systematically plan your course, you can take account of several factors which might require you to be adaptive.

A systematic approach to planning should include consideration as to how the course-room will be used for different learning phases. At the same time, questions should be asked as to the adequacy and appropriateness of the room or rooms available. Is the room large enough? Is it quiet enough? Is it free from distractions? Are other rooms available if needed? How will furniture be used and is there enough (chairs for example)? Where will refreshments be taken, and is it necessary to account in the training plan for time spent travelling to and from parts of the site?

What is the access to the room like? Unless you are sure that there are no wheelchair users attending your course, you will need to check. The same degree of awareness is required when you are considering your exercises and learning activities. If all your exercises require some form of written response, have you considered the possibility that some of your learners might be visually impaired?

Other considerations relating to the learning environment might include such questions as, What arrangements, if any, do you need to make for smokers? Do you know where the toilets are and will you make sure that the learners will be able to find them too? Where will people hang their coats? If it's hot or cold, will the ventilation or heating need to be adjusted? etc.

- What materials will be needed?

When you are engaged in planning a facilitated training course, it can often be useful to take a very broad view as to what learning materials may amount to. To the more obvious provision of marker pens, flipchart paper (or newsprint), easel and writing materials for learners (where you are to provide these) can usefully be added such resources as videos, hand-outs, role-play cards and information sheets, etc. We have also found it useful to include a 'learning materials' column on our training plan, allowing us to note the requirements of each specific exercise or learning activity alongside details of timing, phase development and group structure.

- How the group will work together (group structures).

Facilitated training involves different forms of structured (and at times unstructured) learning activity in which learners are encouraged to interact with each other in various group formations. Unfortunately, group structure isn't always as carefully planned as it should be and may at times be left completely to chance. As with all aspects of training, this issue can have a significant impact on resultant learning in that a careful, considered, and ap-propriate choice and use of group patterns can add to the effectiveness of the learning process itself. For example, following an exercise in which learners-have been exchanging ideas in pairs, it might be more appropriate to re-group them in fours, allowing two sets of pairs to exchange findings, rather than to leap straight back into a plenary session. What is important is that you *plan* for the use of group structures that fit your planned learning for students and which facilitate their efforts. At the same time, it is vital that you project empathy with the learning group at the planning phase, thinking through what you will be asking them to do on the course itself. Is it necessary? Is it appropriate? Is it reasonable? Does it assist learning? Is there sufficient variety? Will learners be able to work with a broad cross-section of the learning group throughout the course?

Pause for Thought

Think back to those occasions when you have had to plan and prepare for a facilitated training course.

- *To what extent did you adopt a systematic approach to your planning?*
- *Did you consider each of the areas we have described?*
- *Are there other issues, not discussed here, which should also be addressed at the point of planning?*

The facilitative decisions reached during this crucial planning phase will often dictate the nature and extent of the learning opportunities available to students during the course itself, either limiting or expanding scope, depending on the choices that are made. To be effective, your facilitation must be built upon a sound training plan that has been developed with due regard to the impact that each planning decision will have on resultant learning, group interaction, motivation and group dynamics. A commitment to Real-world Facilitation starts at this point, a commitment that requires you to question all the facilitative choices that you make in order to ensure that learning is relevant, significant and meaningful to the learner at *every* stage of the facilitative process and that it makes sense and is of use in their real world.

PRE-COURSE COMMUNICATION WITH YOUR LEARNERS

Real-world Facilitation seeks to maximize the effectiveness of the fundamental process by which learners interpret the meaning, significance and usefulness of new information and new ways of approaching and resolving problems, by comparing and integrating these new ideas with existing knowledge, beliefs and recipes for action and problem-solving. Accordingly, it is an approach that leads to deeper, more permanent learning that is directly transferable to typical everyday situations and problems. As the results of a study by Marton and Säljö (1976a; 1976b; 1984) suggest, learners who direct their efforts to capturing the meaning of information and who then make sense of it by relating it to their own understanding, are involved in a 'deep approach' to both the processing and retention of that information.

This fact also leads to an enhanced motivation to learn, as learners quickly realize that ideas, strategies and solutions, formulated during the process of training, have arisen out of direct consideration of the problems and issues that are very much a part of their ongoing real world. Because the main focus of this approach places learning within a real-world context, with all that this entails, it also generates a high degree of learner ownership. Learners find it easy to identify with both content and process, precisely because it is directly relevant to their learning needs outside of the training setting.

The provision of such responsive and relevant training does, however, demand that wherever possible, individuals' learning needs should be identified *before* the course is planned, allowing for the inclusion of learning phases, exercises and activities which are directed towards meeting these stated needs. Ideally, this 'needs-analysis' should be in the form of a short informal meeting between each learner and the facilitator, during which the learner is provided with an outline of the proposed subject areas to be covered and the facilitative approach that will be adopted. The learner should then be asked a series of straightforward questions which seek to uncover learning need. These questions should focus upon real-world issues and problems, encouraging the learner to formulate any learning needs in terms of that practical reality. The following questions provide an example of what we mean:

- What issues arise for you in this area in terms of your day-to-day work?
- What do you consider to be the most important issues that should be dealt with in this area?
- What day-to-day problems and concerns does this area cause for you?
- What skills would you like to develop on the course in order to be better equipped to deal with such issues and problems?
- Other people who will be on the course have identified (*particular issue or problem*) as being important for them; how true is this for you?
- Your sponsoring organization has identified (*particular issue or problem*) as being important; how true is this for you?
- Can you give me some idea how much time we should allocate to each of the issues you have identified as being important?

Pause for Thought

- *Are there other questions you would want to ask a learner during any pre-course tutorial of this type?*
- *What might be the consequences of not contacting learners before a course?*

We fully acknowledge that you may not always be able to find the necessary time for such a face-to-face needs analysis with each of your learners and that you may be able to meet with only a few (if any). Contacting your learners by telephone, although obviously less effective, would still provide a form of personal contact and an opportunity for you to ask them the same questions that you would have put during any informal pre-course meeting.

Should even telephone contact prove problematic for you, then writing to your learners, enclosing a structured needs questionnaire is a possibility. In this case we would recommend that you lay out your questions in such a way as to provide plenty of space for learners to respond effectively without feeling constrained by the space available. A covering letter emphasising the value of learner comments at the pre-course phase should also be included, in an effort to motivate response (it is estimated that most questionnaire surveys yield only a 10–12 per cent response rate!)

Learner resistance

It is not uncommon to encounter learner resistance to forthcoming training during the needs-analysis phase. Some people resent the implication that they *need* training because they are failing in some way. Others may view training as a management 'cop-out' and a substitute for more far-reaching and tangible necessary change. Still others may baulk at the prospect of facilitated training, which (as we suggested in Chapter 1) has at times been labelled and stigmatized. From our experience, we have found that it pays to approach such resistance openly and honestly, acknowledging the validity of learners' reactions, but at the same time emphasizing the practical relevance of the course for each learner and the real-world approach that will be adopted to encourage learning. Make use of the very fact that you are seeking to identify people's own learning needs as an indication of your desire to promote relevant, significant and meaningful learning.

At the same time, there is also a need to be realistic about the stated requirements of the sponsoring organization. Although you may discuss with the sponsor the ways in which you plan to balance organizational and individual learning needs, addressing each, as far as is possible, within an integrated and systematic training plan (as we suggest later in this section), there may be instances in which certain stated learning needs, which have been identified by your learners, cannot be accommodated within your training remit. In order to avoid creating false expectations of what the course may offer your learners, it is crucial that you jointly discuss what can realistically be achieved.

In our view, the person who is usually most aware of the real learning needs of the learner is the learner him or herself. This is an important point to raise with the sponsor, should disparity become apparent between the organization's view of each person's learning needs, as against the learner's personal assessment of those needs. Where possible, we would advocate an approach in which discussions with the training sponsor seek to establish broad areas of training need (through the identification of general issues, problems and concerns), linked with an agreement that specific learning needs within that subject area will be sought from the participants themselves, based upon day-to-day, real-world problems, issues and experiences.

PRE-COURSE COMMUNICATION WITH THE SPONSOR

Unless the training that you undertake is part of an ongoing programme, or is training that you have yourself identified as being necessary within your own organization, it is likely that the person who will first approach you with a view to developing a training project will be a training, personnel, or human potential resource manager, or alternatively, some other person responsible for sanctioning new training. For the sake of simplicity we have called this person the training sponsor.

The choices made and decisions reached as a result of meetings with the sponsor, for the purpose of clarifying organizational requirements, are critical to the shape of any training enterprise that results. As with pre-course meetings with learners, such meetings should be viewed as opportunities for needs analysis, where agreement is sought between the facilitator and the sponsor concerning a wide range of issues that relate directly to the provision of training for learners, not the least of which being a clear indication as to what the organization hopes to achieve by sanctioning this training.

This phase of organizational needs analysis should begin by clarifying why a need for training has been identified and why particular individuals have been chosen to attend. Has this training need arisen out of a recent problem, or cluster of related problems within the organization, or in response to either internal or external criticism? Is it part of a structured development programme, or is there a need to invest staff with new skills because they face new demands? Alternatively, has the training need arisen out of a desire to improve the quality of service delivery? This motivating factor is important as it will say a lot about anticipated learning outcomes.

Having identified why the sponsor perceives that the organization needs the training in question, it is important to establish the nature and extent of that training need and to discuss the likelihood of meeting it (in full or in part). Unfortunately, sponsors seldom realize the time that effective learning takes and may be overly optimistic as to what can be achieved over a given time span. Part of the facilitator's role at this stage of the process is to offer expert advice that is both honest and realistic, without being overly and unduly cautious. There will almost inevitably be a need to re-focus expectations, prioritize, and to clarify realistic and achievable learning outcomes. Take time also to explain the Real-world Facilitation approach to the training sponsor. Emphasize its value as a method that encourages transferable and usable learning that lasts long after the training course has finished. You could also describe its central theme: that of working with, and addressing, a learning agenda constructed so as to balance both the organizational and the learners' self-identified learning needs, placing each within a real-world context and ensuring that ideas and strategies developed within the training setting become directly responsive to the issues and problems they are designed to address.

A necessary but potentially challenging part of your discussions with the sponsor should concern the learners' perceptions of their own learning needs. All too often, training is simply imposed on individuals from above, with little, if any, thought as to whether they themselves agree and identify with that training. Has the sponsor canvassed the views of those who will be attending the course? Do potential learners share the sponsor's view that training is required or that the subject of the training is the most pressing and necessary? Will course members be volunteers?

If the need for training has arisen as the result of a problem within the organization (or a cluster of related problems), you will need to work with the sponsor in order to clarify the potential causes of such problems and how training might help in addressing them. Useful questions in this regard might include:

- What exactly is the problem?
- Who is involved and how have they contributed?
- Is the problem widespread?
- How long has the problem been going on for?
- How might training help?
- Is training the only solution or are there other non-training strategies needed?
- Does the training have other (for example, resource) implications?
- What strategies have been tried and to what effect?

Having worked with the sponsor to identify the broad training requirements of the organization and the general learning outcomes anticipated, it can be useful to suggest that the formulation of a responsive training plan requires that the initial training framework agreed between you should now become 'fleshed-out' in terms of individuals' specific learning needs in this area. To this end, each participant will be approached and spoken with for the purpose of ascertaining their individual learning requirements. Through the involvement of these two groups in the early development of your training plan, you will be able to bring together the ideas of both sponsor and learner, integrating them to form a coherent training structure in which both have ownership and to which both have fully contributed.

AIMS AND PLANNED LEARNING OUTCOMES: PUTTING LEARNING OUTCOMES INTO WORDS

The mere mention of objectives or planned learning outcomes can be enough to irritate those facilitators who see learning purely in terms of discovery through experience. Glance back at the educational opposites diagram (Figure 1.3) and you will get an indication of the position of objectives in educational thinking. We have used the term 'planned learning outcomes' throughout this book as we feel that this phrase accurately reflects our view of the importance of learning as a process which should be directed towards pre-planned outcomes. These outcomes will depend upon the form of training you are undertaking and of the particular learning needs that you are working to meet. For example, a planned learning outcome could direct learning towards the raising of learner awareness of specific real-world issues and problems. Another may seek to encourage a raised awareness of the consequences and implications of these issues, while another may set out to develop new skills or promote the formulation of new ideas or strategies. Although planned learning outcomes are not written in the restrictive language of tight behavioural objectives, they none the less serve to structure the learning process by providing 'learning landmarks', the accomplishment of which becomes evidenced through the nature and level of learner contributions and involvement.

The difference between planned learning outcomes and behavioural forms of learning objectives is an important one and you will need to reflect on the way you formalize your learning intentions in light of this debate. The opposite ends of this debate are exemplified on the one hand by Mager (1984, p.3) who operates firmly at the behavioural end. He notes that,

> an objective is a description of a performance you want learners to be able to exhibit before you consider them competent ... it describes the result of instruction rather than process.

Compare this with the alternative view expressed by Macdonald-Ross (in Curzon, 1990, p.139):

> ... education is an exciting journey, the precise destination of which we cannot know in advance. It recognizes no bounds, it cannot be constrained by paths and marked roads....

Pause for Thought

Having read these two quotes from Mager and Macdonald-Ross and having looked again at Figure 1.3 in Chapter 1 –

- *What do you feel is the most valid approach to the writing of objectives/planned learning outcomes?*
- *In what style are your current planned learning outcomes written?*

If you found yourself reasserting your belief in precisely defined statements of behavioural outcomes, consider how compatible such a position is to a real-world approach to encouraging learning. If, on the other hand, you found yourself unable to accept *any* statement of learning outcome because such statements appear too restrictive and definitive, constraining the freedom to learn, then you may experience further concern that our approach to facilitation necessarily requires that learning should be directed towards pre-planned outcomes. Here are some of the reasons why we have found it important to design and document course aims and accompanying planned learned outcomes:

- They stop you falling into the trap of following a pattern of reactive training in which the process of learning has no clear path to follow.
- They provide a structure for your facilitation.
- They make you accountable. We have noted above that training sponsors need to know what return they can expect from their investment. Planned learning outcomes provide a clear statement of learning intent.
- They will help you to focus and structure your own preparation.
- If formulated correctly, they can help direct learning energy and focus towards identifying and addressing real-world issues and problems and can help in the development of skills and strategies which meet real-world challenges.
- They will help you to gauge whether your training is proving effective.

Some hints on writing aims and planned learning outcomes

- Each should be designed from a real-world standpoint, conforming to the requirements of the relevant planning principles, by seeking to account for, and work with, issues and problems that are relevant and significant to course members.
- Specified planned learning outcomes should be structured so as to openly encourage the transfer and application of learning to real-world situations.

- The number and scope of planned learning outcomes should be realistic and achievable, allowing each major aspect of the course to be dealt with in sufficient and appropriate depth.
- A planned learning outcome should be included that specifically addresses the identification and consideration of barriers to the transfer of learning to real-world situations.
- The course aim and planned learning outcomes should, as far as possible, reflect the stated needs of both the sponsor and the course members.

DEVELOPING AUTONOMY

Many of the key ideas in Real-world Facilitation express the need to look beyond the boundaries of the training setting, to the world outside in which learners live and work. It is from there that they will come when they enter the course-room and it is to there that they will return when the training course has ended. Training must provide continuity between departure from and re-entry to this everyday environment, by recognizing the existing skills, knowledge and experiences of learners when they arrive in the training setting. This existent knowledge, these skills and these current ways of understanding and resolving problems must be drawn upon and made full use of, as they provide the means by which new information, new ideas, new skills and new strategies will become understood, integrated and internalized as workable and usable ways of thinking and acting. At each stage of the training process the facilitator should encourage learners to look beyond their immediate surroundings, testing and validating what they have learnt in terms of its usefulness, fit and viability in that everyday world.

Because the learning group is a transitory resource, a resource that was not available to the learner before entering the training environment and will not be available after he or she has left, it is important that individuals are encouraged to develop levels of effective autonomy on the course rather than excessive reliance on the group. This is a somewhat paradoxical situation as, on the one hand, facilitators quite understandably strive to create an interactive and integrative learning environment in which interdependence and shared insight add to learning opportunities. On the other hand, any reliance on the power of the learning group pushes learners further away from developing the ability to identify and address issues and problems for themselves, precisely the skills they will need when they return to their own real worlds. A way to overcome this is by encouraging each learner to use the group as a source of ideas and alternative perspectives (very much in the way that the learner might draw upon and integrate the thoughts and ideas of others in the world of everyday life), and at the same time ensuring that the learner pursues his or her personal learning projects. The facilitator must remain alert to the ever-present possibility that individual learners may become completely enveloped by the group, losing independence and failing to reach a level of interdependence.

> [Ideally] Individuals pursue their own learning needs within the context of the group, referring to others for support and feedback and for validation of the enterprise. Much learning occurs from interactions between group members. There is an emphasis on democratic decision-making and the consideration of different points of view within the group. The development of the group itself is often a focus for learning, with the aim being for the group to strive towards a relationship among its members that allows individuals to engage in their own learning with the tangible support of others. Interdependence is highly valued (Boud, 1988, pp. 25–6).

In his book *Developing Student Autonomy in Learning* Boud (1988, p. 23) also provides a series of student activities which are consistent with the pursuit of effective autonomous learning (described below). These ideas could usefully be reviewed at the planning stage, providing a form of checking mechanism with which to measure the level of facilitative control being exercised at any part of the course. We would only add the caveat that these forms of learner activity need to be placed within a real-world context so that, for example, any phase which tasks students to '*create a problem to tackle*' ensures that any problem chosen is one which has been drawn from experience, is a problem likely to be encountered again (albeit in different circumstances) and that 'tackling' the problem should mean developing realistic, useful and usable solutions and strategies which are sufficiently realistic to be transferable to that real world.

During a facilitated training course, learners could be encouraged to:

- identify learning needs,
- plan learning activities,
- find resources needed for learning,
- work collaboratively with others,
- select learning projects,
- create problems to tackle,
- choose where and when they should learn,
- use teachers as guides and counsellors rather than instructors,

- opt to undertake additional non teacher-directed work, such as learning through independent (structured) learning materials,
- determine criteria to apply to their work,
- engage in self assessment,
- learn outside the confines of the educational institution, for example in a work setting,
- decide when learning is complete,
- reflect on their learning process,
- make significant decisions about any of these matters, that is, decisions with which they will have to live.

(Boud, 1988)

SUMMARY

In this chapter we have systematically reviewed the application of Real-world Facilitation planning principles to the planning phase of the facilitative process. We emphasized that decisions reached and choices made at this crucial stage serve to create the very context within which subsequent learning takes place and finds meaning. The identification and integration of both learner and organizational learning needs was discussed and we spent some time considering how your training plan can best be structured so as to ensure that it remains responsive to such needs, while at the same time allowing sufficient flexibility to respond to the dynamics of the learning process at the point of training delivery. In the latter part of the chapter we focused on the question of aims and planned learning outcomes, offering guidance on their formulation from a real-world standpoint. Finally, we took a brief look at strategies for developing learner autonomy.

CHAPTER 5

Getting the Group Working at the Right Level

Outline

In this chapter we will start to apply Real-world Facilitation principles to the delivery stage where the trainer encourages and manages learning in a training setting. To ensure that the course gets off to the right start, it is important to think about and apply facilitation tools such as ice-breakers, energizers and group contracts. These in turn will help create a learning environment in which disclosure (an essential element of real-world learning) is encouraged, and can be sensitively and effectively utilized in the learning process.

Planned learning outcomes

After you have dwelt on this chapter for a while, we hope that:

* *You will have considered the application of Real-world Facilitation principles to group ice-breakers, energy levels and group energizers.*
* *You will be able to make meaningful contracts with your learning groups.*

- *You will have thought about the issues which surround disclosure in the light of Real-world Facilitation principles.*
- *You will be more confident in your ability to encourage disclosure, and deal with it effectively when it happens.*
- *You will feel more able to make appropriate disclosures yourself.*

ICE-BREAKERS

The beginning of any facilitated training session is often a tense and awkward time for both learner and facilitator alike, particularly where participants have not met before. This apprehension and anxiety must be dealt with before the group can begin to work together at an effective level, and this is where ice-breakers can be of real use, breaking down initial barriers to learning by introducing people to each other and getting them actively working together.

Ice-breaking exercises form an important part of the learning process. All too often they are relegated from the premier division to the minor league of facilitation as 'bolted-on' afterthoughts; they may even be forgotten altogether. The latter approach seems to be based on the assumption that adult learners can manage this phase on their own, naturally coming together to introduce themselves, find out about each others' backgrounds and so on. The truth is that this rarely happens. This can cause an acute problem where a course or seminar is short. It may be that you have only half a day, or one day, to achieve your planned learning intentions. In such circumstances you will need to get the ice broken quickly to enable the group to move forward in a more relaxed and effective way. Don't ignore the possibility that apparently already formed groups won't have any ice to break. It is our experience that group members who seem to know each other already will often benefit from getting to know each other better. Another occasion when ice-breaking is necessary is where you, the facilitator, are coming into a group which is already formed; you will need to get to know the members, and they you, if a relationship of trust to be formed.

This trust will be important for later learning, and a significant factor in its development will be the breaking down of barriers to honesty and communication which might exist within the learning group at the outset. If carefully planned and managed, ice-breaking can also have the effect of challenging the stereotyping and labelling which can occur in the early phases of a course, the result of people's initial impressions of each other. Lengthy periods of learner inactivity at the outset of the course when a course overview is provided, learning intentions are outlined and a group learning contract agreed, can mean that members of the group have little opportunity or inclination to say or do anything.

An ice-breaking exercise can be just the thing to help them to start to come out of themselves. Of course the type of exercise you run will have a considerable effect on this and later participation and learning.

You need to ensure that any ice-breaker exercises you run are relevant to the group. If they also have some direct relevance to the purpose of the course then so much the better, and this will be made considerably easier if you have planned carefully and found out as much as you can about the learning group beforehand.

> *We attended a seminar aimed at challenging attitudes toward HIV and AIDS. The facilitator started off with an exercise in which we all had a worksheet which was divided into sections, each section containing such categories as: 'a person who reads the New York Times', 'a person who has never been drunk', 'a person who is wearing green', 'a person who knows how to use a rubber (condom)', and so on. Group members had to circulate, and talk to each other with a view to finding out the name of a person who fitted each category on the sheet.*

This exercise was fun, effective, and got the group working well together and all talking. It was particularly effective because it was relevant to the group in two ways. The content was likely to match the realities of the people in the group. There was a high probability that someone in the group would be wearing green for example. Even better, it got people talking about a subject which is normally taboo and often embarrassing, namely, condoms. Delicate issues could be raised at the outset in a very safe non-threatening way, and this was achieved by including the difficult issues from the outset.

For some people, ice-breaking exercises can be significant learning events in themselves. Those who are naturally shy and feel in some way inadequate or overawed by other members of the group can gain early confidence from learning that they can, in fact, talk to strangers quite freely and that the experience is not nearly as daunting as they might at first have imagined. Learners might also be unused to working closely with other people and may find an early and safe introduction to team-building very useful.

Apart from the particular objective of breaking the ice, these exercises should generally be straightforward and, although not shrinking from raising important issues, should generally aim to provide a facility for members to meet and speak with each other in an informal and safe activity, while at the same time introducing aspects of course content. A good rule of thumb to measure whether your ice-breaker is pitched at the right level is whether or not there is a need to feed it back (process it or unpack it); if you do, then the activity is probably pitched too high. An exception to this rule is when you are training trainers. While they are, in one sense, involved in the content, they also need to be able to take a step back and view the exercise for its educational implications.

Some hints on using ice-breakers

- Realize their place in the learning process and their importance in breaking down barriers to learning, group cohesion and communication.
- Keep them active. Ice-breakers can often meet the need for people to introduce themselves, learn about each other's backgrounds and become familiar with names.
- Get the group to brainstorm what they would like to know about each other (keep this at a fairly basic and relevant level) and then make this the basis for a getting-to-know-you session.
- Make ice-breakers work for you by including appropriate issues but at an introductory level.
- Keep them straightforward and explain their use to the group.
- Remember a rule-of-thumb: if you need to feed-back your ice-breaking activities they are probably pitched too high (unless you are training trainers).

ENERGIZERS AND GROUP ENERGY LEVELS

Even when you have been doing something interesting and enjoyable, like reading a good book, after a while your concentration and enthusiasm begin to tail-off. This is often an indication that you need to take a break or have a change of activity – maybe make a cup of coffee or walk the dog. This is also true of energy levels in your learning group which, from time-to-time, may need a boost. This is where energizers come in – activities which offer a change of momentum or direction.

Group energizers can take many forms and you should keep an open mind about which activities might be suitable. They should offer:

- A high degree of learner involvement.
- One or more changes of activity.
- Learners the opportunity for moving around rather than just sitting and talking.

- The opportunity to re-focus the group's attention back on the issues in hand.

A good example would be a quick-fire brainstorm on a new but related subject, which was run in such a way that learners left their seats and recorded their own ideas on flipchart paper or 'newsprint' attached to the wall.

An important aspect of skilful facilitation is the ability to keep in touch with the mood and energy of the group, monitoring its momentum by gauging non-verbal messages, levels of involvement and commitment to the work in hand, by staying attuned to signs that concentration and enthusiasm may be dropping.

Pause for Thought

- *From your experience, identify some of the typical verbal and non-verbal indicators that group energy has fallen.*

Having identified from your own experience a number of indicators of falling group energy levels, compare your findings with those we have listed in Figure 5.1. Remember, at this stage we are dealing only with the problems posed to effective learning momentum as the result of falling group energy levels and not with issues arising out of course content, emotional and interpersonal reactions to occurrences within and between members of the group, or other aspects of group dynamics which might be described as difficult or problematic behaviour. We discuss these issues and the general need for mid-course corrections later in the book.

In the extreme, it is possible for group energy levels to fall so low that the course itself becomes jeopardized. Effectively, the course crashes, and might have to be abandoned.

> *We were once totally unrealistic in our expectations of what a group could handle. We had three hard days of developing facilitation skills and then moved into four further days of learner practice with course participants, facilitating long sessions in pairs. The rest of the learning group provided the audience.*
>
> *On reflection, and having subsequently applied Real-world Facilitation principles to the circumstances, we realize that this was our mistake. Energy levels had been high for the first three days. They then began to flag simply because there was no respite.*

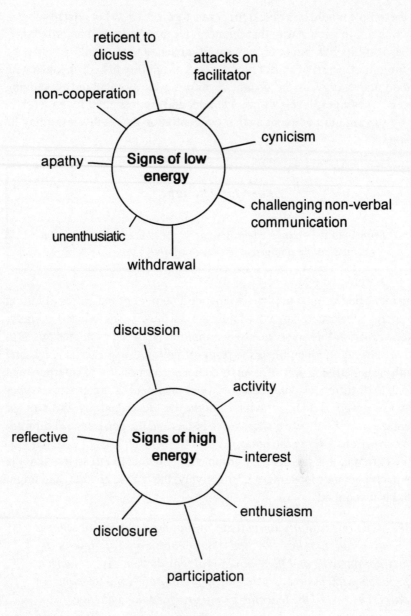

Figure 5.1 *Signs of low and high energy in a group*

The group's sense of loyalty to those members who were doing the facilitating meant that everyone maintained constant pressure. Seven days of this (albeit with a short break in the middle) was just too much. We had been negligent in our planning and had failed to take sufficient account of how the chosen course structure would affect energy levels. In this case we had to call the course to a halt nearly a day early. We had crashed.

Our rather unscientific graphs (Figure 5.2, A–C) illustrate our experience of how energy levels can vary. Figure 5.2(A) illustrates the course we have described in the anecdote above. It started well, the energy peaks and troughs were as to be expected, but suddenly things took a nose dive and the course had to be brought to a close.

Figure 5.2(B) illustrates the sort of energy profile you should expect with a group which is working well. The ice-breaker(s) you choose, and any contract made with the group, should have the effect of stimulating the group into working energetically. After this point it is perfectly normal for the energy level of the group to rise and fall, and this can be due to a number of factors. We have found that it is not unusual for the level to fall after a long feedback session following an exercise. Typically the learners will have been working well; disclosure and lots of supportive group interaction will have been taking place. It would not be unusual for the group to become increasingly reflective until either the facilitator or group member will suggest that a break is taken and the 'spell' will be broken. After such a break the group may need to be refocused with an energizing exercise.

Other typical times for energy levels to flag are after lunch and towards the end of the day. After lunch, a longer energizing activity may be indicated. At the end of the day you may, if it is within your discretion, need to be flexible about the finish time. Failing this you will need to keep energy high enough for the learning to be meaningful. Be aware of the needs of learners in their real world. Your course members may have a bus or train to catch, they may need to pop into the supermarket on their way home or today might be their birthday. Whatever the reason, remember that your learners, like you, have a life outside the group and it plays an increasingly important role in their thinking as the day gets nearer to its end.

Pause for Thought

- *Reflect on a time when you have been in a facilitated learning group. How did your own energy levels rise and fall? How can you account for this?*

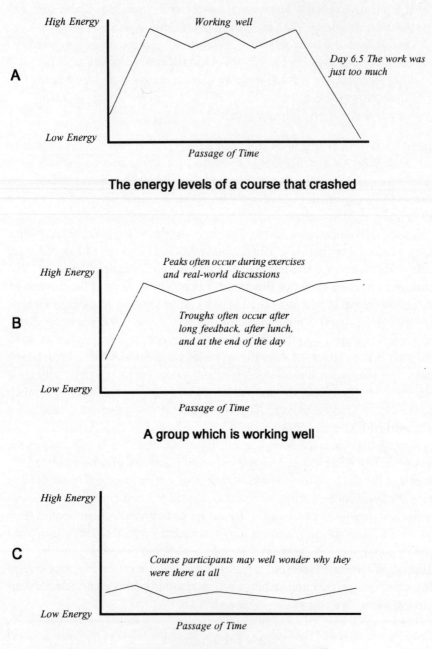

Figure 5.2 *The fluctuations of group energy levels*

Figure 5.2(C) shows a group which has not really got going at all. What energy there is at the outset is not consolidated and built on, and the course simply drifts on. There would typically be a general air of apathy among the learners and it would not be surprising to find cynicism or even resistance. Almost certainly, it would be difficult for the facilitator to encourage disclosure or stimulate effective discussion.

Reasons for the type of energy profile shown in Figure 5.2(C) are many. It is possible that the facilitator might be at fault. Our experience is that such a profile (which of course represents the extreme situation) is usually the result of an approach to the learning that does not key into the learners' real world. Application of the principles of Real-world Facilitation will go a long way to overcoming this. Of course some of the factors are outside the control of the facilitator. Some organizations require their employees to attend courses whether they like it or not, and this can have a very negative effect on their energy. This aspect of the planning phase is discussed in Chapter 4.

Some hints on using energizers

- Keep in touch with the energy levels of your learning group. Watch out for the tell-tale signs of flagging attention, reduced participation and/or enthusiasm.
- Be aware of, and plan for, the times when group energy is particularly low, after lunch for example, or at the close of the day or towards the end of the course.
- Energizers, by their very nature, should be lively, active sessions which provide an opportunity to re-focus and change the pace.
- Avoid the use of games or activities that make learners feel overly self-conscious or silly.
- Try not to confuse discomfort within the group when confronting difficult issues with falling energy levels. Signs of withdrawal or lack of enthusiasm may suggest that learners are trying to avoid challenging aspects of the course.

MAKING REAL-WORLD CONTRACTS

At the start of any training course a certain amount of apprehension in the group may arise, concerning the focus of the course itself and how learning will be encouraged and managed. Learners may need reassurance that their contributions, particularly if these are personal disclosures, will not be rubbished or shut out by other members of the group, for example.

Our everyday conversations with each other mostly work out ok because, on the whole, we conform to certain unspoken rules about how to behave: not interrupting for example, or challenging or testing-out the accuracy of what is being said or claimed. However, when people enter the more formal environment of the learning group, controlled by a facilitator and structured with a view to achieving set aims and planned learning outcomes, there may be a need to clarify and formalize such unspoken social rules. This is particularly true on training courses which raise and confront challenging interpersonal and attitudinal issues involving learner reflection and disclosure. Here, individuals often need a degree of protection against the possible insensitivities or poor interpersonal skills of other group members.

Group learning contracts address this need by placing such issues on a formal footing. They consist of rules, agreed by and binding on the group which, if adhered to, should encourage an open, safe and sensitive learning environment. Timid members of the group may feel protected by a contract, and by the same token the rules contained within it may provide a degree of authority to deal with difficult behaviour should it subsequently arise.

For group learning contracts to be effective and successful they must be realistic, achievable and economical, addressing learner anxiety and group needs without becoming unwieldy or unworkable. Rules agreed should make sense to all concerned, should be phrased in plain and direct language and carry the consensus of the group if possible.

Remember, even though an issue is not dealt with in the contract, it may still be addressed as and when the need arises. It is always better to build a trim, limited contract than to harness the group with pages of rules which seem to set a fearful agenda.

Do:

- Explain to the group at the outset that the fact that something is not covered in the contract does not mean that it will be ignored if it arises and needs addressing.
- Encourage *workable, achievable* and *economical* contracts that include only those rules felt to be essential by the group.
- Insist that contracts are sensibly written, making sense to the group. What is the point, for example, of making a rule about smoking when you are working in a no-smoking building? It isn't negotiable in the first place. This should be your starting point. If things are not negotiable then the group cannot have real control over them. To pretend otherwise will provoke frustration right from the outset.
- Be realistic about what can be agreed. If you are going to make a contract then keep it tight. Three pages of flipchart covered with strange sounding

rules and personal foibles can be very off-putting. For example, is it really necessary to have, as we have witnessed ourselves, a written request to keep the room well ventilated?

- Be sure about the partners to the contract. Is it between you and the group or is it between the group members themselves? Who will monitor the contract? Will there be any sanctions against those who break the rules? If there are to be sanctions, are they really enforceable and what impact will such enforcement have on the learning environment?

- Identify with sponsors or training managers wishing to visit the learning group, the time they will be coming and tell the group this at the outset. Such visits can raise anxiety, causing participants to withdraw, hesitant to say anything which might show them in a poor light to a supervisor.

An early, open and direct management of such visits and the possible reactions they may generate can minimize disruption and lower anxiety. Sponsors will rightly expect the opportunity to see how the course is going, whether this is in order to show their commitment and interest or to gauge the value and impact of the training they have sanctioned. Either way, such requirements tend not to be negotiable so don't be tempted to negotiate them with course participants if this is the case.

In our experience it is useful to encourage the sponsor or manager to join the group and participate in the learning activity, thus minimizing their observer status and maximizing their commitment to and understanding of the course.

Don't:

- Make contracts where they are not needed. We have found that learners can sometimes find contract-making a weary and irrelevant process. They are very aware of the potential disruptiveness of interruption, rubbishing others and so on and may well resent the implication that a contract is needed to prevent it. It might be better in such circumstances for you to deal with individual instances of this behaviour as it arises (we suggest strategies later).

- Pretend things are negotiable when they aren't. Start and finish times are normally fixed, particularly where vocational training is involved. You may have some discretion in this but if you haven't, then you can't allow the contract to ask for this.

- Be naive about confidentiality. Of all the ingredients of contracts we have seen, this has caused the most aggravation. A group member might well ask for confidentiality, knowing full well that others are likely not to respect it. Raise these potential problems with your learners and encourage them to think about confidentiality in the context of the real world of the learning group and, more importantly, the real world of everyday life both inside and outside the work environment. Consider these questions:

- Is confidentiality necessary? If yes, to what extent?
- Confidentiality from whom?
- Confidentiality about what?
- Confidentiality for how long and in what settings?

Remember, it is crucial that each aspect of the contract should be realistic, workable, achievable and understandable.

- Don't use language that people cannot readily identify with. It is very common for a request to be made for 'I statements'. We take this to mean that people should speak for themselves. Now that is fine – people *should* only speak for themselves when they are vocalizing feelings. One person cannot possibly know what another is feeling, without being told, or without making sure that the inferences being drawn from non-verbal communication are correct.

  The problem is that when such entries are made in contracts, they are often misunderstood and nearly always broken. With such ambiguity at the outset, the course can be slow to take off.
- Don't try to sneak in your own rules while pretending they are from the group. You are most likely to fall into this trap when attempting to be neutral, on the face of it not steering the group in any particular direction, but subconsciously really wanting, or perhaps needing, to.

Figure 5.3 contains a brief summary of the main points about making contracts.

IDENTIFYING REAL-WORLD ISSUES AND PROBLEMS

There can be little doubt about the importance of getting the learning group working at the right level from the outset of any training course. Your choice and use of ice-breakers, the management and facilitation of any contract-setting phase and the need for ongoing monitoring of group energy levels and their control through the use of energizers will all have an impact on how quickly this happens.

But what actually is the *right level*, and how will you know when you have encouraged your group to reach it? Through the systematic adoption of Real-world Facilitation principles these questions become easier to answer. It is the point at which learners start to disclose (either to themselves or others) and confront relevant issues, problems and experiences that arise within their own

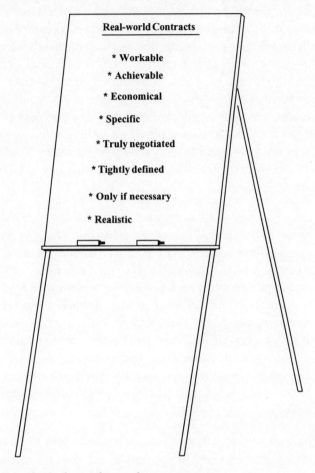

Figure 5.3 *Things to think about when making contracts*

real world and begin the process of addressing and resolving these through the formulation of realistic and achievable strategies and commitment to necessary change

The relevance of such issues, problems and experiences will depend upon what the aim of the course is. For example, on a course designed to address difficulties in dealing with customer complaints, the facilitator would need to encourage early identification of the real problems, issues and experiences facing group members when they are involved in aspects of real-world customer complaint resolution. This could be achieved by involving learners in exercises and learning activity which allows them to progress from broad identification of general factors, such as organizational policy, to more specific, individual factors such as their own skills in handling disputes and their own attitudes and behaviour towards types of complainants.

Such identification produces a form of learner agenda which can and should provide the basis for later work. Although it is crucial that such real-world issues, problems and experiences are identified at the outset, it is necessary to take learners *beyond* this disclosive stage towards the point at which they begin to confront and address identified issues and problems, reflecting on the validity and real-world consequences of their attitudes and behaviour before finally working on realistic and workable strategies for dealing with them *where it counts* in the real world of everyday life beyond the learning group.

> *While running a staff development training course on equal opportunities and fair treatment issues, we were surprised at the speed at which real issues can come out. The group came to the course knowing each other quite well already, and we knew them. At an early stage in the course we ran a quick ice-breaker exercise which asked participants to describe something that had happened to them in the last 24 hours under the three categories: 'trivia', 'trauma', and 'treat'. One of the female course members described something trivial, and then said that her trauma was that she had yet again faced sexism in the staff-room and that she was not sure how much longer she could put up with it. We had got right to the heart of a real issue about equal opportunities almost without trying.*

The thing about this is that such a disclosure cannot be ignored. Treat it as a facilitator's gift! You now have a real-world issue which can act as a spring-board for later learning. Be careful not to lose it. Some follow-up may be necessary if you are to make the most of what has happened. You could also use this disclosure as part of an agenda-setting process with the group as we have said, or possibly as a means of refocusing on an existing agenda.

Do not leave the identification of real-world issues, problems and experiences too late; they should provide the very elements which your group will be working with during the course. You can think of it in terms of a real-world **PIE**, the ingredients of which are real-world *Problems, Issues* and *Experiences*. At each stage *get* the real issues out, identify the real problems and *always* get the learners to share real examples of how this affects them in their everyday lives. This process of identification leads us into an area of facilitation which is fundamental to experiential learning, that of disclosure.

DISCLOSURE

One sure sign of a positive beginning to a training course will be that the group is starting to discuss and disclose. One reason we find facilitation to be such a useful learning medium is that unlike, for example, being involved in distance learning, learners on a facilitated course have an opportunity to vocalize their feelings, thoughts and attitudes in a way that enables and encourages reflective learning. The act of vocalizing is often called 'disclosure', and in the remaining part of this chapter we will be discussing some of the issues that relate to it.

Disclosure is a vital aspect of our facilitation model and involves individuals unearthing their own experiences, revealing their opinions and attitudes and describing their behaviour. Then, often with the help of the group and guided by the facilitator, the learners are encouraged to make sense of their experiences, reflect on the validity and appropriateness of their disclosed attitudes and to understand the consequences of their behaviour, turning this into valuable and usable learning.

Pause for Thought

- *When you have been involved in facilitated learning, what factors have encouraged you to disclose to the group?*
- *When you disclosed your own experience to the group, what did it feel like?*
- *What factors might prevent you disclosing to a learning group, either as the facilitator or as a learner on a facilitated course?*

An important point to be made here is that disclosure is not an end in itself. This is so for several reasons. Its usefulness for learning will depend on the type and depth of the disclosure being made, as well as a recognition that disclosure of itself does not necessarily lead to learning. It is all too easy to fall into the trap of thinking that because the group is 'bubbling', 'motoring', 'steaming', 'interacting' or whatever adjective is used in your arena for a group which is discussing well, that learning is necessarily taking place. People can and do disclose for many reasons, and in the real world these may not always be helpful to the progress of the group.

In assessing student trainers we have often had to correct an assumption voiced during feedback, that a good discussion on the face of it meant things were going well for the lesson. The proof of this fallacy is particularly evident when groups are split up and asked to discuss independently some topic or other. A tour round the group with a cocked ear can often be a sobering time for a facilitator! Even the most professional groups have been heard discussing the basketball results, last night's TV or even more deflating, the quality of the facilitator, when it had been assumed from all the outside evidence that they were discussing their attitudes towards and experiences of the topic of the lesson. So how can we recognize when disclosure is taking place? This can be neatly illustrated with an anecdote from a trainers' course in equal opportunities which we ran.

> *In order to encourage early identification of real-world problems, issues and experiences concerning the facilitation of equal opportunities training, we had tasked a group of experienced trainers to identify three statements or expressed attitudes with which they would find difficulty in coping had they been made by a learner on one of their own training courses.*
>
> *This was a very useful exercise because it encouraged group members to reveal areas of equal opportunities that they needed to think through or to develop their own skills.*
>
> *During the course of this exercise, one member of the group stated that he had not been able to think of anything, then, almost as an aside, he said, 'Mind you, I would have great difficulty doing any training about gay issues, I mean, I think homosexuality is wrong isn't it, it's as simple as that'.*

Clearly, this learner was disclosing a fairly deeply entrenched view. The evidence was there:

* The subject matter had relevance both to the person disclosing and the course we were running.
* The individual displayed common non-verbal signs of a disclosure which he found uncomfortable to reveal. There was a certain unease, a slight squirming on the chair, averted eye contact and a slightly quivering voice.

While this was a useful disclosure it could not be left there, because disclosure is not an end in itself; the individual, the group and the facilitators were left with more work to do.

Using this incident as a worked example we have provided a possible structure which would allow the facilitator to take the learner beyond the initial disclosure towards a point at which change was possible. We must assume that at all stages the facilitator is operating with a high degree of awareness and sensitivity and that the need to encourage learning is balanced with the need to support and protect the learner.

Feelings
- How does the person feel about holding this view?
- How does he think others might feel, knowing he felt that way?
- How might one of his learners who was gay feel about his views?

Real-world Consequences
- What are the implications of this view for his role as a trainer in equal opportunities?
- How compatible is this view with a commitment to fairness for all?
- How will he work with a learner who vocalized a similar view to his own in a training setting?
- How will he work with a learner who vocalizes an opposite view to his own, supportive of gay and lesbian rights and needs?
- How will he work with a learner who professes himself gay?

Sensitive Challenging
- How valid is this view?
- Is it based on contact with gay people?
- How would the person challenge this view for himself?

Change
- Does the person want to change?
- What are the barriers to change?
- What might assist change?
- Who will support change?
- Are strategies for change achievable, realistic and workable?

Establishing the real-world consequences of such a view, thinking about realistic and achievable future action and encouraging commitment to necessary change are crucial components of the facilitation of learner disclosure, if learning is to become translated into action outside of the learning environment.

Disclosure can occur at a number of different levels and for a variety of different reasons, some more helpful to the learning process than others. This factor must be borne in mind by the facilitator when encouraging learners to identify problems, issues and experiences in the area being addressed, as the type, level and motivation of disclosure will dictate the way it should be responded to.

Helpful disclosure

- *Disclosure which leads to learning.* This occurs when learners are openly and safely sharing their experiences and feelings with the group with a view to making sense of them and considering real-world consequences and implications.

- *Disclosure as a means of cleansing.* People often need to get things off their chest and really appreciate the opportunity to off-load some of the tensions which may have been building up in them over a period of time. Anger might be a part of this, and a degree of venting may take place, perhaps about management, lack of resources, frustration about lack of equality or whatever. Don't forget, when this happens, seek out the real issues and problems and get the learner to give examples. That way it makes it easier to go beyond the disclosure and start to develop strategies for necessary change.

- *Disclosures which amount to a cry for help.* As we have stated several times already, and will repeat throughout this book, your learners will bring with them all the problems and pressures which crowd in on us all. Learners do not just switch off from them because they have come into a learning group. Treat this experience as your raw material with which to work. Whilst we in *no way* suggest that Real-world Facilitation can be equated with psychoanalysis, there is a sense in which learning through experience and the disclosure of that experience, can be seen as therapeutic for the learner.

- *Disclosure as illustration.* Often learners will use a degree of disclosure to illustrate something they are trying to explain to the group. For example, a person who is trying to explain how it feels to be on the receiving end of prejudice might choose to disclose about a situation in which they themselves had been a victim. This is very valuable disclosure, providing lived experience to describe an important issue.

Unhelpful disclosure

- *Disclosure to be the centre of attention.* This is quite common and needs to be watched out for. It can be quite an irritant to the rest of the group and they might well expect you to do something about it. In the real world, time constraints may well be such that you will not have time to get to the core of the person's need to be the centre of attention.

- *Disclosure for the purpose of manipulating the group or facilitator.* This occurs, for example, when an individual says something like, 'I was only saying that to wind the group up' or, 'I said that because that is clearly what you want to hear'. Such an attempt at spoiling or manipulation can be very damaging if not dealt with carefully, particularly as the disclosure may have been real enough but the qualifying remark purely defensive.

- *Disclosure which has no bearing on the purpose of the course.* This is a particularly tricky problem because it often seems to occur with people who are inexperienced in learning through facilitation. The disclosure itself may be genuine, but the problem for the facilitator is that it tends to blur the way forward. Should you stay with the disclosure (which is way off the point) and risk losing the group, or should you risk alienating the learner and keep the group focused on the true business? In real-world terms the latter is probably the most likely course of action, although you will want to make sure that you get alongside the individual at the first opportunity and check that they are not smarting too much from not having their contribution valued.

The depth of disclosure is another issue to be considered. There is little point in encouraging learners to reveal their deeply held convictions on, say, religion, if the purpose of the course is to develop ways of dealing with difficult people on the telephone. Be aware of your plan and purpose and ensure that your encouragement aims to generate useful and usable problems, issues and experiences which bear directly on the subject being dealt with. If learners are able to see that the things they reveal in a training setting lead them to achieve relevant, meaningful and significant learning which is directly translatable to their everyday situations, they will be far more willing to participate in the course at a truly effective level.

Some hints on facilitating student disclosure

- Encourage the disclosure of real-world problems, issues and experiences which bear directly on the subject of the training being undertaken.
- Choose and use exercises and activities which encourage learners to raise their own real-world problems, issues and experiences as the very content of such learning activity. (An example of this is provided in the anecdote above which sought learner identification of equal opportunities issues they would find difficulty in coping with as trainers.)
- Only encourage useful, usable and relevant disclosure which will serve to promote meaningful, relevant and significant learning for group members.
- Try to place disclosure into the learners' context. One way of achieving this is to consciously ask the learners for examples from their own experience, of what they mean.
- Consider recreating learners' real-world experiences within the training

setting through role play, perhaps encouraging them to 'play themselves' if they are happy to do this.

On an assertiveness course for trainers, one of the learners disclosed that she could never enter a classroom without feeling a strong sense of nausea and nervousness. The course leader asked her to recreate the context several times by entering the room in which the training was taking place. She reflected on each occasion and realized that part of the problem was that in the very act of entering the room she was trying to take on an unnatural role instead of being herself. This was meaningful, significant learning for her, and as we were all trainers, it had relevance for us all. It was Real-world Facilitation in action and it worked.

- Go beyond disclosure by encouraging learners to reflect on the consequences and implications of attitudes and behaviour revealed.
- Be aware of the possible effects of the exercises you use. Think ahead, imagining how you would feel and react if asked to undertake such an exercise ... don't be tempted to ask your learners to do something you yourself would not do.
- Be aware of your own level of confidence and experience in facilitating disclosure at different levels.
- Remember the time you have available to fully process disclosure.
- Keep in mind the necessity to balance the needs of a particular learner with those of the learning group as a whole.

There are some excercises which can, if not handled carefully, generate an aftermath which is potentially very difficult to cope with. Johari's Window is an example of such an exercise (in Boshear and Albrecht, 1977). This self-image exercise aims to raise each learner's awareness of how he or she sees him or herself and how others see them. Participants are asked to identify one negative and one positive attribute in respect of each person in the group, recording their views on a form provided for the purpose. Following collation of these forms, participants are then told what others have said about them and are asked to reflect on this feedback, paying particular attention to any similarities which might be apparent.

During subsequent feedback, learners are encouraged to think about such issues as the difficulties associated with accepting criticism (both good and bad), the extent to which self-image is reliant upon the views of others, and the disparity which can occur between their own view of self and the views of others. While on the one hand this exercise can be an extremely powerful tool for raising self-awareness, it has also been known to cause considerable distress and anxiety because it was not handled well by the facilitator.

We know of two learners, one male and one female, who were involved in a Johari's Window exercise early in a long training course. The facilitator read out to the whole class the positive and negative points which had been recorded about each class member. The male learner had to listen nearly 20 times to his negative characteristic as being his acne. The only good characteristic most people in the group felt worth noting about the female on the other hand, was the (large) size of her breasts. Both learners suffered considerable distress and had to be counselled by an experienced tutor to help them get over the experience.

Such mishandling of an exercise by a facilitator can be at best damaging, and at worst perverse. Be very careful that you operate within the limits of your own ability to sensitively guide and protect your learners. In addition, ensure that you use exercises wisely and with purpose.

Pause for Thought

- *Take some time to look back over the Real-world Facilitation delivery principles in light of what we have discussed regarding disclosure.*

Confronting

In the very act of encouraging learners to identify their own learning needs through the disclosure of relevant problems, issues and experiences from everyday life, you will create an agenda which your learners rightly expect you to work with. Some of the matters they raise may prove challenging to you, but it is vital that you do your best to confront necessary and relevant issues head on.

By this we mean that you should not adopt the type of avoidance strategies which might characterize the behaviour of some of your learners. On many occasions we have witnessed facilitators avoiding issues by choosing to ignore the obvious implications of something which has been said, pretending not to notice the non-verbal signals which indicate a real issue for the learner, or generally being so rooted in a pre-set agenda that the raising of real-world issues is either unwanted at worst or at best unnoticed.

A practical way to confront issues is to encourage the learner or the learning group to consider the consequences and implications of their view, attitude, belief, feeling or whatever it might be that has been disclosed. This is a particularly useful strategy when something has been said with which you personally disagree. It often happens in equal opportunities training! Identifying or reflecting back the consequences of a particular position can help to illuminate it for the learner and it avoids the possibility of your becoming embroiled in an argument with the learner(s). If you do that, you might as well pack up and go home.

Overall, it is our experience that where courses have got off to a good start with relevant ice-breakers, sound, meaningful contract-making and sensible opening exercises, then disclosure will happen naturally. If you have applied the Real-world Facilitation planning principles to your pre-course work and then follow these through to the initial delivery stage, it is highly likely that you will have successfully got the learners working at the right level.

SUMMARY

In this chapter we have outlined some of the dos and don'ts of making real-world contracts. We noted the importance of ice-breakers and energizers in getting the group working and helping it to stay working. We suggested that a fundamental aspect of Real-world Facilitation is to identify the issues and problems which learners have and get them to give examples from their own experiences.

Disclosure was discussed as being a core aim of facilitated experiential learning, and we identified both helpful and unhelpful forms of disclosure. We finished by linking some types of disclosure with the problem of avoidance, a topic we will deal with in the next chapter.

Chapter 6

Maintaining Group Momentum

Outline

Despite careful planning and preparation, and even though the initial stages of a course have gone well and learners have begun to work at the right level, there are still many things that can occur within the group which can frustrate effective learning as the course unfolds. In this chapter we will be focusing on such barriers, offering hints and strategies to help you recognize and deal with them as they arise. In a similar way to a pilot having to take account of the effects of turbulence in maintaining altitude, a facilitator must acknowledge and resolve forms of behaviour in the group which can threaten group momentum.

Planned learning outcomes

By the time you have read this chapter we hope you will have a better understanding of:

* *The learner comfort zone and its effects on learning.*
* *The facilitator comfort zone and its consequences for learner motivation and subsequent learning.*
* *Forms of avoidance, their identification and impact.*
* *Real-world strategies for dealing with such avoidance.*

*The main focus of this section therefore, will be a detailed consideration
of two important facets of facilitative training:*

The comfort zone
— *What it is.*
— *Recognizing the comfort zone.*
— *How it relates to effective learning.*
— *Moving out of the comfort zone.*
— *Barriers to moving outside it.*

Avoidance
— *Its various forms.*
— *How to identify avoidance.*
— *What motivates avoidance.*
— *Its consequences for effective learning.*
— *Dealing with avoidance.*

THE COMFORT ZONE

Let's face it, none of us likes feeling uncomfortable, especially in a group of
people, some of whom we know and perhaps work with on a day-to-day basis.
Normally, people feel safe in the knowledge that their views, opinions and
beliefs will remain unchallenged, hidden from view or simply taken at face
value. Although they may underpin our ways of thinking about and behaving
towards others, our beliefs, opinions and attitudes seldom become the focus of
our own or others' attention. We generally feel comfortable in the knowledge
that, by-and-large, people will take us as they find us.

This is not the case within the learning environment, particularly on courses
which deal with issues such as interpersonal behaviour and relationships, or
those that consider equal opportunities and fair treatment. Likewise, training
in assertiveness, management, team-building and many other similar subjects
is bound to include exercises and learning activities which are designed to
encourage personal reflection and disclosure of learners' views, thoughts and
feelings on important and often contentious issues.

Feelings of safety and security can and do evaporate as learners are
encouraged to step outside the anonymity of everyday relationships into the
stark and revealing area beyond this comfort zone. This is the reality of being
a participant on a facilitated training course which aims to encourage learners

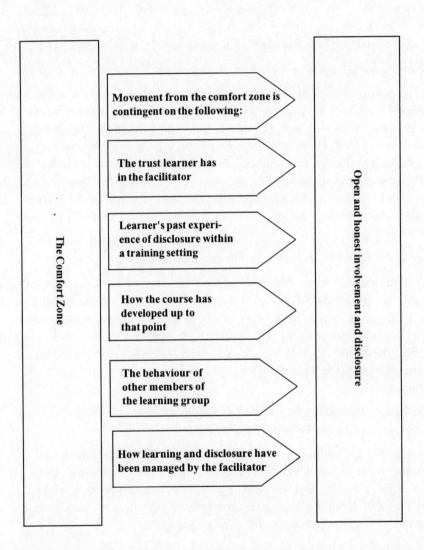

Figure 6.1 *Factors which influence movement of the comfort zone*

to disclose, consider, and then begin to address real and pressing issues (see Figure 6.1).

When learners are asked to reflect on their own views, feelings and past behaviour in this way and to discuss these issues with the learning group, various thoughts and concerns about the topic under discussion can emphasize vulnerability and heighten anxiety for some learners. Here are a few examples.

- *'Fear of having my views attacked or questioned'.*

Stepping outside the comfort zone requires the learner to take risks by disclosing his or her views on the subject under discussion, or describing his or her experiences or real-world problems to the learning group. By doing so the learner chances having his or her contributions questioned or tested by the facilitator or by other group members. Fear of having opinions, attitudes and past behaviour scrutinized in this way can lead learners to adopt various strategies which limit disclosure and effective participation in the learning process; in short, strategies which insure against venturing outside the comfort zone.

- *Lack of conformity with accepted or encouraged values ('I don't agree').*

Where individuals realize that they are out-of-step with the expected or accepted viewpoint, they may feel isolated and fearful of saying what they really think on the topic. This anxiety can be demonstrated most particularly in equal opportunities training where disclosure of prejudice can lead to the individual becoming labelled as racist or sexist by other group members. In such circumstances the typical strategy is to withdraw in an effort to stay safe and comfortable.

- *Lack of commitment ('It's not an issue/big enough issue ... I don't feel strongly ... I can't get worked up about it').*

Staying inside the comfort zone can also allow learners to hide a lack of commitment on issues which if revealed might cause embarrassment. A learner might consider that their apathy toward company values might be better left undeclared for example, especially if members of management and/or supervisors are present in the learning group.

- *Feeling of risk taking ('Too much of a risk ... I'm not ready').*

Some learners find the prospect of disclosing their opinions and feelings a daunting prospect, especially in a strange group. Such feelings of discomfort and vulnerability can represent a real barrier to involvement at anything other than a superficial level.

- *Fear of being misunderstood despite support for accepted or encouraged value ('I can't express what I want to say and it might come out all wrong').*

Unlike everyday encounters, what people say in learning groups is often subject to unaccustomed scrutiny. Conversations tend to be focused on important issues and the progress of the group rests on the useful contributions of the group members themselves. This puts an onus on participants to put their viewpoint clearly as they will invariably be judged on what they say by both the facilitator and others within the learning group.

Learners are aware of this fact and it may push some to say little or stay safe, not necessarily because they hold views they would rather not reveal to others, but because they find it hard to explain their position clearly. If they have been misunderstood in similar situations in the past this is even more likely. This can be another good reason to seek refuge in the comfort zone.

- *Fear of alignment with unpopular 'standard bearers' ('I don't want to be associated with them even though I agree with their position').*

In some organizations the working culture encourages cynicism towards certain issues such as professional ethics or quality of service. Even though members of the learning group may actually subscribe to the professional values of the organization, they may choose not to openly admit this for fear of being associated with unpopular standard bearers (ie, those that openly express support) or of losing credibility in the eyes of their peers. Again, such anxiety can lead to participants firmly staying put in the comfort zone, where they keep their views quietly to themselves.

- *Lack of knowledge ('I should know').*

Another concern which pushes learners to stay safe is a perceived lack of knowledge about something the learner feels he or she should know. To limit embarrassment they may choose not to join in until the danger of exposure has passed.

- *Lack of skill and its associated embarrassment ('I should be able to do this').*

As with a perceived lack of knowledge, learners who fear that a lack of skill might be exposed to the group may likewise 'duck-and-dive', skirting issues, not contributing, participating less or at a lower, less effective level.

- *Embarrassment at disclosure ('I don't feel comfortable telling others/showing others what I think or feel').*

Within the framework provided by Real-world Facilitation, personal disclosure should occur at the level that is necessary to identify relevant, real-world issues, problems and experiences. Even though this should limit unnecessary probing it may nonetheless create embarrassment or anxiety for learners who have not been used to sharing their views and experiences with others.

- *Too hard ('Too much like hard work, I prefer an easy life/ way out/ option').*

While we like to think that the training courses we run stimulate and encourage learners to participate, the reality can sometimes be that certain individuals aren't prepared to work too hard and would rather sit back and blend in with the furniture. Here the comfort zone is more to do with ensuring an easy time.

Pause for Thought

- *From your own experience as a learner or facilitator, can you identify other reasons why learners seek the safety of the comfort zone?*

Identifying comfort zones

Part of a staff development course for established trainers, which aimed to improve the skills involved in the facilitation of equal opportunities courses, required participants to take it in turns to assume the role of the facilitator for the purpose of running learning exercises with the group, all of whom were peers and experienced and skilled facilitators in their own right.

The exercise that we were asked to lead was a hard-hitting, disclosive activity that encouraged participants to place themselves at a position on a line (imagined to be running down the middle of the classroom floor). The ends of this line represented the two extreme positions on the topic and were identified by pieces of flipchart paper attached to the wall and labelled appropriately. By placing themselves at a particular position on the line, learners were able to indicate where they stood in relation to either extreme and in relation to each other.

On this occasion we were focusing on the trainers' commitment to identifying and addressing issues of racism in their lessons, when these issues arose out of discussion on other matters. The two extremes entered on the flipchart paper at either end of the room were: 'Totally committed/Always address' and 'Totally uncommitted/Never address'.

However, before we could start the exercise by asking participants to stand on the line (having already encouraged them to reflect on their approach in such circumstances) some members of the group began to show discomfort. This became more apparent when one participant asked for an explanation of terms used in introducing the exercise: 'What did we mean by racism?', 'What did we mean by commitment?'. Their non-verbal communication suggested that they knew only too well what the terms meant.

This is a good example of learners displaying reluctance to leave the safety of the comfort zone. Even though most participants were happy to accept that, as with all facilitated learning, words and terms carry their usual everyday meaning, the strategy of questioning detail deflects attention away from the central proposition of risk-taking involved in the exercise and the disclosure it encourages and facilitates.

There are of course many different ways in which learners will indicate to you that they wish to remain comfortable and safe; a few are listed below as illustrations:

- Outright refusal to take part, eg, 'I simply don't want to discuss gay rights!' or, 'I am not getting involved in that exercise, it's silly'.
- Apparent reluctance to take part, displayed either verbally, or more likely non-verbally, eg, avoiding eye-contact with the facilitator, adopting closed body position, etc.
- Questioning the validity of the exercise or topic being discussed.
- Questioning the need for the exercise or the need to cover that topic, eg, 'Is it necessary to talk about empathy, can't we get on?'
- Questioning detail (as illustrated above).
- Involvement, but at a safer, less disclosive or risky level.

An example of this occurred on a recent course. We asked participants to identify questions or statements which they as facilitators would find difficult to deal with if confronted with them by learners in a training setting. Most participants came up with real concerns: 'I find it daunting when a learner asks me to my face if I have been racist, or if I am still racist' or, from another learner, 'How do you answer a male learner who says honestly to you that some jobs are better dealt with by men than by women?'. Such contributions say a lot about where these learners are in relation to the issues they are struggling with and represent a degree of personal risk-taking.

In contrast, others within the group made safer contributions: 'I don't like it when learners are late to class', or, 'I can't really think of any questions or statements to be honest, I suppose I could say when learners ask stupid questions'. These contributions don't reveal much about the learner's real-world problems, issues and experiences and do not involve any real risk-taking.

- Flighting, ie, laughing off a serious issue, making a joke rather than giving an honest and open response.
- Asking a question of the facilitator rather than answering one.

Pause for Thought

- *From your own experience can you identify other examples of how learners indicate to you that they wish to remain in the comfort zone and attempt to resist personal risk-taking in a learning setting?*
- *Have you as a learner ever felt a desire to stay within your own comfort zone? If so, what was the issue, and how did you try to stay safe?*

Willingness to move out of the comfort zone will be contingent on several factors, some of which are within the control of the facilitator; these often include:

- The trust that learners have in the abilities, commitment and integrity of the facilitator as they have come to know him or her up to that point.
- Learners' past experiences of moving out of the comfort zone in other training courses.
- How the course has developed up to that point. If it has been carefully and thoughtfully planned, with sufficient flexibility that encourages learners to disclose at a safe and comfortable level early on, while encouraging progressively more opportunity for individuals to identify significant real-world issues as the course unfolds, then learners will be more inclined to move outside the comfort zone and stretch themselves through appropriate disclosive risk-taking.
- The behaviour of other group members. On courses where the general trend is to get stuck in and to make the most of learning experiences

offered, learners will be more inclined to accept the learning environment as safe and the sharing of opinions, attitudes, experiences and issues as less of a personal risk.

- How learning and the interactions which underpin it have been managed by the facilitator. Where learning has been sensitively and effectively handled, with due emphasis on its relevance, significance, meaning and transferability to real-world situations, learners will be more inclined to participate fully and at an effective level.
- Personal willingness to disclose. Of course, many participants will come to your courses only too willing and motivated to get the most out of them. This might be particularly so if you have conducted effective pre-course tutorials, and the learner has already done some preparatory thinking.

The facilitator comfort zone

Feelings of safety and security are an important part of confidence; it is therefore not surprising that even as the facilitator you will experience instances where you deal with your own vulnerability in front of the group by staying in your own comfort zone. In addition to the behaviours described above, the facilitator has an additional armoury of strategies which can be called upon to keep safe and these can arise at any stage within the facilitative process.

At the planning stage you can choose a learning plan, each component of which ensures that you are operating well within your own safety limits. Risky exercises or other learning phases can be excluded without others noticing or alternatively can be made the responsibility of a co-facilitator. By picking and choosing what will become included in any training course with an eye towards your own comfort, you are of course planning in part to meet your own needs. This may not always be a conscious process. Accordingly you should pause to reflect on the way you plan and prepare with a view to identifying and addressing the choices you make and the reasons behind them.

At the point of course delivery you have access to many other strategies which allow you to steer the group away from areas you would rather not deal with in depth.

In a recent case, the facilitator, a professional self-employed trainer, would constantly push the group along in the name of good time-keeping whenever participants started to discuss issues and problems in depth, disclosing their own personal experiences with the group: 'That's an interesting point but if we dwell on that we won't be able to get through today's timetable'; 'We'll come back to that if we have time after the next exercise', etc.

Although time-management is an issue to be considered when working with groups, it must obviously be balanced against the learner's need to identify and address issues, experiences and problems which the course has revealed to be significant for group members. Where, as in this case, the call to move on coincides with those parts of the course which lead to the heart of important and challenging issues, learners may rightly begin to question the commitment and capabilities of the facilitator.

And, in another case:

Learners undertaking a long residential course in equal opportunities found the facilitators only too happy to stay firmly within the comfort zone of imparting information, but reluctant to move into the realm of discussing feelings and fears. Likewise, learner frustration rose when attempts by the group to relate the application of the knowledge they had been given to their own training role were curtailed in favour of even more theory input by the course leaders.

In such circumstances the facilitator's feelings of discomfort and vulnerability brought about by the prospect of having to move into a 'high-risk' area are dealt with through the imposition of the power that the facilitator has over the learning group, the power to stick to or change direction, to dismiss a line of discussion as unimportant or untimely, or to move into a new activity phase.

Learners are rarely blind to this manoeuvring and may use it to validate their own reluctance to stretch themselves by undertaking disclosive forms of activity or other risk-taking. Alternatively, it can lead to a build up of learner frustration and cynicism which itself becomes a significant barrier to further learning.

It is often said that as a facilitator you should be a good role model, encouraging learners not only to do as you say but also to do you as you do. It follows that where you work to promote effective learning by encouraging your learners to identify real-world issues and problems through reflecting on their own experiences, you, the facilitator, must also be ready to confront those issues and problems, working with your learners through the challenging stages of considering consequences and building workable strategies and solutions. By turning away, at any stage, you will fail to meet the very learner needs you have worked to expose.

Whether it is your own or your learners' comfort zone that you are considering, it is important that as a facilitator you remain aware of the many reasons why any of us might seek refuge there. Likewise, you should keep in mind the various verbal and non-verbal indicators that might suggest that a learner is resisting involvement in an aspect of the course that he or she finds challenging and risky. In the same way that you constantly (often unconsciously) monitor the dials on your car dashboard when driving, you should constantly (and, eventually, almost unconsciously) monitor the faces, body positions and contributions of your learners when facilitating, picking up clues as to their involvement, commitment, motivation and progress.

We have found it useful to share the idea of a comfort zone with learners as a means of encouraging them to think about their own strategies of resistance and avoidance. Further, it can be helpful to suggest that they monitor themselves (and, if appropriate, each other) for instances when they actively seek refuge there. If done with care and sensitivity, the facilitator can also reflect back to learners aspects of their behaviour which indicate that they are playing it safe and the consequences of this for effective personal development.

AVOIDANCE

Staying put in the safe, known and familiar comfort zone, is certainly one means by which learners avoid having to confront and deal with real and significant issues and problems which impact upon the real world of everyday life. In many ways the image of a comfort zone can be likened to an umbrella, shielding the individual from exposure to new and challenging ways of both looking at and dealing with existing issues and problems. In this sense, strategies of avoidance serve as the vehicle by which learners seek either to remain within or return to the comfort zone and in ceratin respects may actually represent the defensive walls of the zone itself.

In the above sections on the comfort zone we began to identify some of the verbal and non-verbal clues which, to the facilitator, can suggest learner avoidance and resistance. This theme now needs expanding to account for other strategies of avoidance that facilitators can experience within the training setting:

- *Obvious silence.*

The learner remains silent and uncommunicative in a way that suggests a hesitance to get involved and a resistance to disclose. Even encouragement by the facilitator may fail to assist participation. Withdrawal from the learning process has taken place to the extent that the learner won't contribute at even the verbal level.

- *Tone of voice.*

Whether aggressive, hesitant, cynical, dismissive or jocular, the learner's tone of voice suggests that they are trying to avoid addressing the issues being focused on or expressing their opinions on the subject.

- *Gestures – both facial and body.*

Non-verbal indications of avoidance may include lack of eye-contact, looking away (particularly down at the floor), shifting about on the seat, hiding the mouth with a hand, pretending to read a document with great interest, tapping and fidgeting, sitting back with arms (and maybe legs) crossed.

(*Note:* It is always worth remembering that subtle non-verbal behaviour is easy to misunderstand and should only be used as a guide which requires supporting indicators. It can be a mistake to assume that actions necessarily speak louder than words. Also, cultural differences can frustrate accurate interpretation of the meaning of gestures and other non-verbal messages.)

- *'We' statements*

  A female learner talking in a training session said, 'I'm sure that I can talk for all the women in this room when I say that people are being too sensitive about sexism. Generally, women don't mind the attention men pay them or when blokes try and find out if you're wearing stockings and suspenders ... it's just harmless fun'. The facilitator then turned to the other women in the group and asked them if this was a fair comment. One replied, 'I resent her talking on my behalf as if she knows what all women think. I do find such behaviour offensive, it undermines my claim to being an equal professional when it happens in the workplace. I think she should be bold enough to speak for herself and not hide behind the rest of us'.

This is a good example of a learner trying to avoid a situation in which she would have to express her views as her own and accept other people's reactions to them. 'We' statements are often used in this way to enforce the viewpoint being expressed by giving it the weight of common opinion.

- *Scapegoating/transference*

Another, often complex, avoidance strategy arises when learners seek to avoid accepting conclusions which challenge their existing ways of seeing the problem by transferring blame onto the victim: 'It's not surprising that Asian people aren't accepted in this country, they make no attempt to integrate', or, 'Black people wouldn't get such a reputation for being criminals if they didn't hang around on street corners'; also, 'Women want equal rights then they go off and have babies half way through their career'.

- *False concern for process*

Another strategy for avoidance involves learners trying to steer the course away from an area which is uncomfortable or challenging. Calls for a break to smoke or stretch the legs, or a sharp reminder to the facilitator of the content of the day's training as outlined in any introductory overview, are examples of this.

- *Identifying with others*

A situation can arise in which a learner's contributions amount to a persistent agreement or identification with the thoughts of others: 'I entirely agree with that argument; in fact John has basically put into words what I was thinking', and the same learner later: 'I think you were right to disagree, your point is well made'. It is probable that we have all done this to a greater or lesser extent on courses and it can often happen that others do argue in the same way that we would have, had we had the floor. The point here is that such agreement and identification with the thoughts of others can represent a strategy through which some learners avoid ever having to make an original contribution of their own, thus escaping from the prospect of disclosing their viewpoint for consideration by other group members.

- *Ridiculing others' contributions*

This can often occur non-verbally where learners give each other sideways looks when a particular view is expressed with which they feel uncomfortable or disagree. Similarly, discrete smiles and almost imperceptible nods, false yawns, shakes of the head and other non-verbals can be indicators of learners resisting the challenge of accepting or thinking through potentially significant learning. Such messages can suggest disdain, either for the point of view being offered or the contributor making it (or both).

Pause for Thought

- *Can you identify other instances of learner avoidance from your experience, either as a facilitator or as a learner on a facilitated training course?*
- *What are the likely consequences, on both individual and group learning, of not addressing such avoidance?*

Facilitator avoidance

We have already identified the ways in which facilitators might attempt to stay securely within the comfort zone and those tactics described are equally applicable to any consideration of facilitator avoidance. Various strategies, both at the planning and delivery stages, can be employed by the facilitator to ensure that the course doesn't stray into 'difficult' waters. These include such things as 'designing out' challenging issues by choosing 'safe' exercises and learning activity, while at the same time restricting the amount of flexibility inherent in the plan itself. We further identified avoidance strategies at the point of delivery such as an unnecessarily rigid adherence to the learning plan and its suggested timings, resulting in learners being moved on at times of facilitator vulnerability. A number of other facilitator avoidance strategies can be added to those already mentioned, including:

- Focusing on members of the group felt to be 'safe' by the facilitator, ie, those who won't ask difficult questions, or make contentious contributions.
- An unnecessarily rigid adherence to the stated course aim and planned learning outcomes as a means of cutting off particular avenues of discussion.
- Arguing that something isn't important when the truth is that it is too challenging.
- A deliberate refocusing of the group through a change of activity when it becomes clear that the outcome of the current exercise will be difficult to facilitate.
- A move away from activity-based learning to more didactic input such as mini-lectures or showing a video for the purpose of re-establishing control.
- Not following up on contributions that might lead towards issues the facilitator would rather avoid.
- Ignoring the non-verbal signals from group members which clearly suggest avoidance.

Facilitator avoidance is an uncomfortable fact that must, like those in any real-world problem, be acknowledged and its consequences considered. It is only then that the problem can be addressed through the formulation of workable strategies which are sufficiently realistic to be effective in the real world of the training setting.

Dealing with avoidance

Strategies of avoidance, if left unchecked, create significant barriers to effective learning. You will recall that the leading principle of Real-world Facilitation suggests that:

Learning should be relevant, significant and meaningful to the learner *at every stage* of the facilitative process. It should make sense and be of use in the learner's real world.

To meet this principle it is essential that real-world issues and problems which are significant and representative for the learner become identified at the outset, forming an agenda which is then addressed as the course develops. Such identification requires disclosure. It follows that avoidance strategies which seek to enable the learner to resist such risk-taking frustrate this important process, resulting in little to work on that is directly relevant and meaningful to the learning group.

We suggest a five-point plan (see Figure 6.2) for dealing with avoidance which is sufficiently flexible to account for and address many of the avoidance strategies described in this book and others you may have experienced or studied.

1. Noticing.
2. Interpreting.
3. Addressing.
4. Allowing feedback.
5. Encouraging involvement, disclosure or risk-taking.

1. Noticing

The most fundamental step in coping with avoidance is being aware of it and this can be hard work, especially in a large learning group. It requires you to concentrate on the group process at all times, keeping in touch with both spoken and unspoken messages and the nature of interactions between learners. At the same time, you must gain a feel for the group dynamic, remaining alert for the various indicators of both avoidance and refusal to leave the comfort zone.

Such monitoring must become integrated into your work with the group to a point where it is not noticeable to participants – a daunting task which gets easier with experience. Take time to capture the subtle, almost hidden messages which can sometimes accompany learners' contributions or their reactions to the contributions of others. At other times the indication of avoidance may be more overt so it is equally important not to overlook or ignore the obvious.

By staying in touch with the learning group you will also notice changes in the level of contributions by particular learners: some may withdraw having

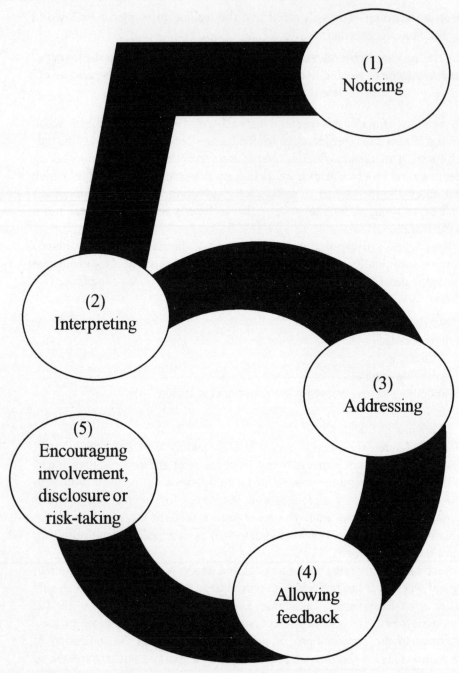

Figure 6.2 *The five-point approach to dealing with avoidance*

previously contributed well; others may not have ventured out of the comfort zone at all, favouring silence.

2. *Interpreting*

Although the act of interpreting behaviour which might amount to avoidance can often occur straight away in the form of a 'gut-reaction', your initial assumptions about what the behaviour may mean probably lack conscious reflection. There is a very real risk of jumping to conclusions and labelling forms of verbal and non-verbal behaviour as avoidance when this might not be the case; a learner may appear hesitant and even reticent but far from avoiding a challenging issue, may in fact be grappling with it, and working through its implications.

Take care to think through exactly why you have formed the impression that a learner is showing signs of avoidance. What are the messages you have picked up on? Is there a possibility that you have wrongly interpreted them? Are there alternative reasons for the behaviour – tiredness or overload for example? You may also want to consider what the apparent cause of the avoidance is. Are you moving into a more demanding part of the course where you might expect some learner resistance?

Although it is important not to jump to conclusions it is equally important not to dismiss signs of avoidance, by convincing yourself that there is probably another explanation. Even though this allows you to continue facilitating without addressing the issue at the time, the consequences for learning and learner participation will compound as the course unfolds, particularly if the developmental nature of the learning plan means that work undertaken later in the course is likely to be even more demanding. Addressing avoidance can be uncomfortable for the facilitator and you should be aware of your own potential for avoidance in this area of your work.

If you are working with a co-facilitator or a recorder, it is a good idea to discuss issues of learner avoidance together. If you have both picked up on the same behaviour and interpreted it as avoidance, it is less likely that a wrong conclusion has been drawn. At the same time, conferring will allow you to discuss alternative meanings or the possibility of some form of personality clash.

3. *Addressing*

As with the concept of the comfort zone discussed earlier, it can often prove useful to open up discussion about avoidance with participants at the outset of the course. The group could be encouraged to brainstorm different avoidance strategies and the way they reveal themselves, before moving on to a general consideration of the consequences of avoidance for their own learning and the group process. By doing this you can build in an agreement, often suggested by learners themselves, for involvement in the learning process at an effective level and a commitment by individuals to monitor their own behaviour.

If avoidance becomes apparent as the course develops, the facilitator could address the issue with the group in a non-specific way (ie, not identifying individuals or describing certain behaviour). This could be done by explaining aspects and examples of avoidance and its implications to the group in broad terms, while at the same time encouraging people to participate at the most honest, open and effective level by stressing the importance of learner contributions to the learning process. To enable learning to become relevant, significant and meaningful it needs to draw upon learners' real-world issues, problems and experiences. Explain this to the group and ask them to reflect on ways in which avoidance frustrates this important process.

At times it may be necessary to address instances of avoidance directly with individuals in order that their behaviour can be explained to them directly. If this is done carefully, the very process of raising the learner's awareness of how their behaviour is perceived by others may be enough to overcome the barrier and encourage more open involvement. Judging whether this should be done within the group setting or on a one-to-one basis during a break is not always easy.

If you choose to deal with an individual's avoidance at the time and within the group, you will retain the context which gave rise to the behaviour and will be able to use the work that you do with the learner as part of the more general learning process involving the other learners. Also, it will encourage others to reflect on their level of commitment and involvement. At the same time, however, you do risk focusing on the individual while amongst his or her peers and this may increase anxiety and heighten the suggestion of confrontation. Unless handled skilfully this could do more harm than good. Conversely, addressing avoidance at a later time, whilst safer, is less meaningful and less relevant to the issues being discussed. A further consideration is that other members of the group who may have encouraged the learner to both accept and deal with the avoidance identified by the facilitator, will not be on hand during any one-to-one conversation after the event.

Addressing avoidance at the time can be achieved at a number of different levels. At the most extreme, you might confront the learner with his or her own behaviour directly, offering an interpretation of it from your own point of view.

On one course, the facilitator noticed that whenever the group began discussing a key issue or began considering the implications of particular attitudes or experiences, one learner withdrew from the discussion, not only through not contributing, but also physically, by sitting back in his chair, doodling in his book and avoiding eye-contact.

The facilitator attempted to draw the individual into the conversation by asking for his views on the matters being discussed and by asking whether he had experienced similar concerns to those being expressed by other members of the group. This had no effect. Choosing an appropriate moment, the facilitator said to the learner, 'David, it seems to me that every time the group begins discussing important issues you push your chair back a bit and start doodling, as if you would rather not get involved; is the discussion difficult for you?'

The learner, faced with this direct question, admitted that he found some people's views challenged his own ways of thinking and this made him feel a bit uncomfortable. He had not been aware that his behaviour was so obvious and although for some time after the challenge he continued to sit back, following a break his involvement grew and with it his personal learning. At the close of the course he said that taking a full part in group discussion had felt quite risky but had been well worth it.

At a less confrontational level you may choose to address avoidance by using carefully thought out observations: 'You appear a little uncomfortable with that idea', or, 'Is this a difficult area for you?' Alternatively, you may choose to disclose to the group: 'I find this a difficult issue and I can see that other group members might feel the same way. Let's be bold and deal with it head-on'. Another strategy can be to involve the learner at a safer level initially by asking him or her to summarize the discussion for the group, this may make it easier for him or her to share their views or experiences with the group when asked immediately afterwards to do so.

Building a safe learning environment in which learners are prepared to disclose issues, problems and experiences which are important to them and to address difficult and challenging ideas, is an essential, if demanding, part of facilitation. Where the group members are clearly working at an effective level it can help to tell them things are going well and to reward individual disclosure.

We were encouraged by the effect of such reward on members of a learning group when, during a good session, several learners had described experiences in which they felt their own behaviour had contributed to a difficult encounter in the workplace. By identifying to themselves and others how things had gone wrong, they were able to consider how their behaviour had contributed, and the consequences of the incident for all those involved. This led to the group being able to formulate alternative strategies which could have been useful and usable in such a situation, role playing each one to gauge its effects.

We told the group how helpful such individual contributions were, and briefly summarized the learning the group had drawn out of the experiences described. The impetus remained high for the rest of the course, forging a general group commitment to exposing and dealing with live and real issues which enabled significant and transferable learning to take place.

4. Allowing feedback

Learners often need space to respond when their avoidance is reflected back to them by the facilitator or other members of the learning group. This reaction may be defensive, whereby such learners try to justify their resistance to involvement or attempt to explain the behaviour away. Alternatively, they may clarify their behaviour and show that it did not amount to avoidance and has been wrongly interpreted. At times you may find that learners react with hostility, particularly where they are unused to training which requires their involvement at the disclosive level. Some, of course, will accept what has been said and admit resistance (as was the case in the illustration above).

This is an important part of addressing avoidance, and should not be glossed over in favour of pushing ahead. When responding, the learner is thinking through what has been said and may be answering doubts that arise in his or her own mind as much as replying to the facilitator. As such it is an important learning process which, even if defensive, dismissive or hostile, may take the learner onward and keep the subject of involvement at the forefront of his or her thinking. At the same time, other group members will be reflecting on their own involvement in the learning process and comparing their own behaviour with that of the learner with whom the facilitator is working at that time.

5. Encouraging involvement, disclosure or risk-taking

However the learner responds, it offers the facilitator a good and appropriate opportunity to reinforce the fundamental importance of individual involvement and its relationship to subsequent learning. If learners want training that meets their needs, which is transferable to and useful within real-world situations, much flesh on the bones of the content of the course must come from the learners themselves. How else can it be ensured that the topics and issues discussed are directly relevant, significant and meaningful to the course members undertaking the training?

The old adage that learners will get as much out of a training course as they put into it is particularly true of Real-world Facilitation for, unless learners describe the shape and nature of their existing experiences in the area being discussed, the facilitator cannot offer a bridge between present and new ways of thinking and behaving which might otherwise be revealed during the course. In effect, the 'known' part of the 'learners' bridge' (see Figure 1.1) as described in Chapter 1 (the area of knowledge, skills, experiences and ways of looking and thinking about everyday issues, experiences and problems which the learners bring with them to the training course) will not be revealed, and ways of linking in new ideas and therefore new ways of dealing with existing situations and problems will not be possible.

CHAPTER 7

When Things Go Wrong

Outline

There are many things which can make a facilitated session go wrong. These can range from problems signalled by simple non-verbal messages, to full-scale attacks on the facilitator (although not, we hope, literally). We begin this chapter by trying to identify the nature of difficult behaviour and explore ways of staying in touch with, and aware of, both group and individual behaviour. This will mean constant monitoring of the information available, picking up on signals and making sense of them. We also take a look at some of the strategies available for dealing with situations which arise, including the need to balance individual and group learning needs. The chapter concludes by considering your own vulnerability as a facilitator.

Planned learning outcomes

After you have read this chapter we hope that you:

- *Will be able to identify the possible causes of certain difficult behaviours in groups.*
- *Will have considered ways of staying in touch with what is happening in the group.*

- *Will have considered some strategies for dealing with difficult behaviour as a facilitator.*
- *Will have developed an awareness of the issues surrounding your own resistance and vulnerability when working with groups*

WHAT IS DIFFICULT BEHAVIOUR?

If you were a teacher in a school, or a parent, you may believe that the answer to this question was fairly simple! School teachers and parents alike confront difficult behaviour on a regular basis. As a facilitator of adult learning, you will also confront behaviour that will be problematic, either for you, the group, the individual involved, or maybe even the organization sponsoring the training. It is important to ask the question, 'What is difficult behaviour?' at the outset, because there is often a tendency to assume that all behaviour which appears difficult is necessarily driven by bad motives. This is not always the case, for either adults or children, although that is not to say that difficult behaviour is never founded on bad motives – it might well be – and we will say more about that later in the chapter.

For the most part however, we need to consider difficult behaviour more in terms of the following:

- *Its challenges to our skills as facilitators.*

At no time during a training course will the attention of the group be more directly focused on the facilitator than when difficult behaviour arises. Although the facilitator's primary role within the group is to encourage and enable learning by providing guidance and support to group members, this role also demands an ongoing responsibility to manage the safety of the learning environment, so ensuring that individuals have the space and opportunity to discuss and address issues, problems and experiences which are important to them.

Learners will expect errant behaviour which obstructs this crucial process to be dealt with in a way that ensures continued trust in the facilitator's skills and abilities to maintain an effective learning atmosphere. In other words, they will expect the facilitator to address difficult behaviour, but in an appropriate and supportive way.

- *Its effects on individual and group learning.*

In respect of its effects on the group, difficult behaviour may include any

123

aspect that might be considered as 'dysfunctional' to the learning process, in that it pulls attention and energy away from the work in hand, causing the facilitator to divert resources toward dealing with the problem that has arisen thus interrupting the group's concentration and focus.

- *Its effects on group dynamics, learner involvement and the learning environment.*

Certain forms of difficult behaviour can be upsetting for other group members, and can have an impact on the energy levels and degree of involvement. Learning groups build up a sense of identity out of the experiences and encounters that take place as the course unfolds. Where this process is punctuated by instances of individual resistance, non-cooperation, cynicism, or any other type of difficult behaviour, the effects on the group dynamics, involvement and support must be considered and accounted for.

- *Its consequences as a form of disclosure.*

Many of the forms of behaviour that are discussed in this chapter arise as a reaction to the challenges and risks posed by facilitated training which encourages the identification of learner's views, experiences and problems through personal disclosure. Even though such behaviour can seem irritating or threatening to the facilitator or a challenge to his or her leadership of the group, its source and explanation are important ... Why is the person acting in this way? What is causing this behaviour? ... Who is it directed against? (You may find it useful to review Figure 3.3 in Chapter 3 which offers a systematic way of working through various types of issues, from the point of identification, through a consideration of their consequences, to the point at which solutions and strategies are formulated.)

- *Its challenge to the authority of the facilitator.*

This is not to say the facilitator is an authority figure to be obeyed at all costs, but with the role comes an implied authority to help the group to work through the learning agenda. If this implied right is challenged by some sort of difficult behaviour, it can prove an uncomfortable experience for the facilitator.

- *Individual and group needs.*

Whether difficult behaviour is interpreted as a form of disclosure, a challenge to the authority of the facilitator, or as in some way disruptive to the learning process, the fact remains that it must be addressed by the facilitator to prevent its negative consequences having a prolonged impact on eventual learning. In the real world of the training setting, this means that the facilitator must focus his or her attention on the person whose behaviour is problematic, and away from the course agenda and other learners.

Care must be taken that in such situations an appropriate balance is struck between the immediate needs of the individual and those of the learning group. On the one hand, time spent dealing with the difficult behaviour could be well spent if, as a result, it allows both the person and the group to move on at an even more effective pace. Even when the facilitator is working with one individual in such circumstances, other learners will be thinking and reflecting on what is being discussed, and may learn things about their own viewpoint and approach to learning as a result. Conversely, if an appropriate balance is not struck, others within the group may become restless and frustrated at the lack of progress, and may resent time spent with one learner if this appears excessive (particularly if this is not the first time that such one-to-one facilitation has been necessary with the same student).

This will mean that in order to balance group needs with individual needs, occasions will arise when you are forced to move on even though the incident has not been dealt with as fully as you or the learner involved might have wished. Strategies to minimize the consequences of this decision include having a tutorial with the learner during a break or at the close of the day; working with the learner for a short time while the group is engaged in a learning activity or exercise; or, if you are working with a co-facilitator, arranging for one of you to work with the learner outside the group if this is appropriate.

Pause For Thought

- *In the next section we will consider ways of staying in touch with difficult behaviour. Before we do, think for a moment about times when you have experienced difficult behaviour as a facilitator or as a group member. How, and in what ways, did you become aware of it?*

STAYING IN TOUCH WITH GROUP BEHAVIOUR

Given its obvious character, it might seem strange that it should be necessary to discuss ways of monitoring and staying in touch with difficult behaviour. However, it is necessary for the facilitator to keep in touch with, and to closely and constantly monitor the learning group, for a number of reasons:

- To monitor energy levels, so that the group members are kept working at

125

their most effective level without overloading them, allowing necessary breaks and changes of activity.

- To ensure that the learning process responds to learner's needs and abilities, by watching for signs which suggest lack of comprehension, confusion, or which suggest insufficient progress.
- To capture opportunities for maximizing relevance, significance and meaning, by picking up on signs of comprehension, realization, enthusiasm and understanding.
- To watch for signals which might suggest learner avoidance or withdrawal to or refuge within the comfort zone.
- To stay alert for instances of difficult behaviour by, or between, group members, which might frustrate the learning process.

Although most types of difficult behaviour (see Figure 7.1) will be obvious to both you and the other members of the group, it must be acknowledged that the first subtle, almost imperceptible signs of it may already have been ignored or missed by the time it becomes fully apparent. It is all too easy to get so fully involved in the learning process and course content that early signals of friction between learners, or messages of unease, or learner withdrawal, etc. pass unnoticed by the facilitator only to reoccur later with greater clarity and immediacy. At the same time, instances of facilitator avoidance can mean that early indications are purposely ignored, in the hope that an uncomfortable challenge might be avoided. This of course seldom, if ever, happens.

Unearthing, considering, addressing and resolving learners' real-world problems, issues, and experiences, is challenging and demanding for both learners and facilitator alike. The closer a topic of group discussion gets to a learner's experience of his or her own real world, the greater that challenge becomes, as the risk of disclosure involves consideration by the learning group of the appropriateness of the learner's current views and past behaviour. Because Real-world Facilitation sets out to maximize the relevance, significance and meaning of learning, by systematically drawing on that learner's real world, it follows that the challenge to the learner is significantly greater in this kind of training as is the associated potential for strategies of avoidance and difficult behaviour.

Accordingly, the Real-world Facilitator must constantly be aware of the increased possibility of avoidance and other forms of difficult and problematic behaviour, and must develop the ability to keep in touch with what's going on within the learning group at all times. As we said in Chapter 6, this can be a daunting and demanding skill which only becomes easier and more instinctive with experience.

In Chapter 6 we offered you a five-point plan (see Figure 6.2) to deal with

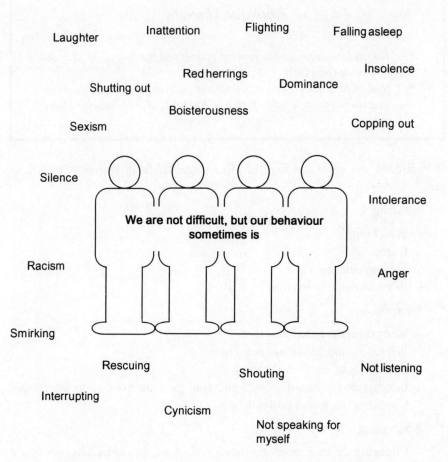

Figure 7.1 *Areas of difficult behaviour that you might encounter*

instances of avoidance. The systematic way of approaching that particular problem is equally useful and valid when watching for and addressing other forms of difficult and problematic behaviour.

Pause for Thought

- *Take a little time now to remind yourself of the five-point plan de-scribed in Chapter 6.*
- *How closely does the plan fit with your current approach to dealing with avoidance and other forms of difficult and problematic behavi-our?*

In summary, our approach involves five stages of facilitator activity. These are:

- Noticing

  - Watching.
  - Listening.
  - Feeling/sensing.
  - What does the behaviour look like?

- Interpreting

  - What does the behaviour mean?
  - What does the behaviour amount to?
  - Possibility of error or stereotyping.
  - Is it directed or non-directed behaviour (ie, conscious or unconscious).
  - Checking out with a co-facilitator.

- Addressing

  - Choosing the most appropriate way of addressing behaviour.
  - Choosing the correct time.
  - Raising the problem with the group or individual.
  - Working with the learner.
  - Balancing individual and group needs.

- Allowing feedback

  - Allowing for response and/or clarification.
  - Giving the learner space to think about their behaviour.
  - Allowing others to think about the problem.

- Encouraging involvement, disclosure or risk-taking
  - Offer involvement/disclosure as a way of overcoming behaviour.
  - Re-emphasize importance of involvement to issue of relevance.
  - Remind the learner of consequences of behaviour on learning.

DIFFICULT FOR WHOM?

In any consideration of difficult behaviour, it is important to establish who is affected by the behaviour in question, as this will have consequences for the way in which the problem is interpreted and addressed by the facilitator. Four possibilities present themselves.

The group

The most obvious and immediate effects of difficult and problematic behaviour are on the group itself. We have already noted that such behaviour can frustrate group progress by focusing attention away from the course agenda and content, leading to the possibility of group frustration. Learners will look to the facilitator to address the issue in a supportive yet economical fashion, using facilitative methods which reflect (and role model) good practice and good interpersonal skills. Failure to act appropriately (or act at all) may be seen as weakness or indecision on the part of the facilitator, and this in turn will erode confidence that he or she is capable of effectively guiding the group through the process.

> *On one occasion the progress of the whole learning group was arrested by one individual and a facilitator's reluctance to deal with the situation. The course was on experiential learning methods, and one group member clearly held unrealistic expectations of what the course was about. This was in part due to the lack of clarity with which the course was introduced. The learner wanted to use the course as a means of therapy for certain personal problems, and frequently broke down in tears. The person's needs were of course valid, but they had no hope of being addressed within the framework of the course in question. The facilitator, who was anything but systematic, spent so much time working with the individual that the rest of us on the course wondered why we were there at all.*

The individual

Although addressing different forms of difficult behaviour within a training setting is a challenging and, at times, uncomfortable part of a facilitator's role, it should be remembered that such behaviour can have a direct and significant impact upon the learner. Admittedly, some learners, particularly those unused to facilitated training which demands disclosive involvement, will be unaware of their behaviour, being ignorant of the fact that they are butting-in, or shouting down, hogging the floor, or being argumentative, etc. Others will be aware of what they are doing and of the fact that it is problematic to the group. It is important that you differentiate, where possible, between learners whose behaviour is conscious and those for whom it is unconscious, as this will affect the way in which you work with them in order to address the behaviour in question.

> *One individual, a particularly forceful character, emphasized everything he said by raising his voice and adopting other non-verbal gestures which appeared aggressive (eg, when speaking he placed his feet firmly on the floor, wide apart, thrust his chest out, leant forward and either pointed with a finger or used violent chopping movements with his hand). These actions seemed to be an attempt at reinforcing the accuracy and validity of his point of view. This behaviour was quite disruptive to other members of the group, who would groan, tut, and shake their heads whenever he made a contribution. We tried to address the problem by describing the verbal and non-verbal elements to him, and by encouraging him to question how others might react to his behaviour. Other group members were also asked to contribute their own feelings and to suggest alternative ways for him to behave. Unfortunately, he was unprepared to accept feedback and dismissed it as an attack on his views.*
>
> *As the course progressed we formed the conclusion that his strength of feeling tended to make him a target for the rest of the group, and this definitely impeded his ability to listen.*

The organization

Difficult behaviour by a group member can indirectly become a problem for the organization that has sponsored the course (or the organization to which that group member belongs). It is paradoxical that such difficulties might well be traced back to the effectiveness of Real-world Facilitation itself. The reason for this is that, among other things, the model emphasizes the need to:

- draw on the everyday experiences and situations of the learner;
- confront issues and problems as they do or may arise for the learner.

In so doing, the facilitator will encourage group members to disclose often deeply felt views and concerns, some of which may have uncomfortable implications for the organization they are representing. Revelations about poor communication or ineffective management for example, while real and genuine contexts within which the learner's day-to-day problems arise, may not be what the company wants (or thinks it's paying) to hear!

This problem centres on the facilitator's divided loyalties between encouraging free disclosure from learners, and staying within the bounds of what is considered acceptable to the sponsoring organization. In seeking options for action, one thing is quite clear: it would be unethical to encourage learners to freely disclose, and then to apply sanctions to them when they do, should their disclosure prove to be uncomfortable for their organization. Conversely, pretending that this problem doesn't exist at all seems to us an equally unacceptable strategy for the facilitator.

We have facilitated courses aimed at forwarding company values and ethos as expressed by that organization's mission and equal opportunities statements. Any statements made by learners (within the learning environment) which are in open defiance of these values, need to be confronted, if for no other reason than because in the real world, such individuals, if so at odds with the organizations they belong to, will have some difficulty in surviving.

This is a difficult area for which there is no one correct approach or strategy. The following ideas may assist however:

- When working with the sponsor or training manager to identify organizational learning needs, raise the issue of feedback from course participants which might suggest the need for organizational change. Will the organization be responsive to well-founded and accurate feedback?
- If you are unwilling or unable to deal with behaviour which will be difficult in organizational terms, you should say so and cater for it in any opening contract.
- Be honest with learners from the outset; if certain aspects of organizational life are not up for grabs, say so, and agree to focus energy where it will be most effective.
- Learners often attempt to avoid confronting their own behaviour by transferring blame on to the organization, its rules and structure. Work with them to separate organizational problems and issues from individual ones.

131

- Where it is unlikely that necessary organizational change will be possible, try instead to encourage learners to effect necessary changes by developing workable and usable strategies within the current arrangements, where this is possible.

The facilitator

To conclude this section on those affected by difficult behaviour let us consider the reactions of the facilitator. Not everyone reacts in the same way: where one facilitator cannot bear the thought of silence in a group, another might quake at the thought of having to cope with an angry group member. The pause for thought below might help you to determine what constitutes difficult behaviour for you.

Pause for Thought

- *If you have experience of facilitating groups, what behaviour do you find most difficult to deal with? What is your nightmare scenario?*
- *Think of a time when you were a learner in a facilitated group and another member displayed difficult or problematic behaviour that you were glad you didn't have to deal with. What happened?*

As a Real-world Facilitator you will want to remember that it is usually the behaviour that is difficult and not the person. Accordingly, it is often better and safer to base your initial interpretation of what the behaviour means on the presumption that it is non-directed, in other words, is not purposefully designed to be difficult or obstructive. This will offer you the flexibility of raising your learners' awareness of difficult behaviour, encouraging them to think through the consequences of it and then formulating ways of overcoming or dealing with it. Should this approach not overcome the problem it then becomes necessary to work with the learner to address behaviour that appears consciously disruptive and designed to frustrate the learning process in some way; in these circumstances a more challenging and confrontational approach may be necessary.

So what specific behaviours are we dealing with? The difficult and problematic behaviours we have noted below have been gleaned mainly from three sources. First, from our own direct observations and experiences of facilitating groups (this has been the main source). Second, from our participation as learners, and having reflected on our own behaviour (Yes! we have ourselves behaved in ways which, on reflection, must have been problematic for the facilitator.) Third, from ideas generated by facilitators in training, who have identified their own 'nightmare scenarios' in groups we have run. A more complete list is given in Figure 7.1, but in the next section the most commonly occurring, and in some ways most difficult, have been isolated and we will explore these in a little more detail. The principles and strategies, however, are broadly transferable to each type of difficult behaviour, and this is illustrated in Figure 7.2.

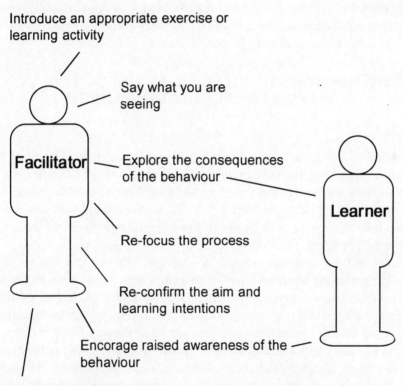

Figure 7.2 *Some strategies for dealing with difficult behaviour which are transferable*

As you read through the various strategies offered, consider their appropriateness to your own approach and ways of working with learning groups. Those that seem more workable and achievable will probably be those that suit you best at the current time. Try other strategies by all means, but bear in mind the possible consequences of experimenting on your learners. Remember also that these strategies represent facilitative action at point three of our five-point plan, ie, action taken to address the difficult behaviour you are confronted with. Before this point is reached and action is taken, it is crucial that you have fully identified the shape and nature of the behaviour in question and have interpreted its meaning, clarifying in your own mind what consequences it has for learning, for the group, and the process generally. After you have worked with the learner or the group to deal with the problem, you should also follow on with the other two important stages, those of allowing for feedback, where you think this would be helpful and appropriate, and then encouraging and enabling involvement at a more effective level.

SOME DIFFICULT BEHAVIOURS EXPLORED AND COPING STRATEGIES IDENTIFIED

Silence

In a world of noise, many of us seem to have become uncomfortable with silence. It is not surprising then, that in a training setting it can become a difficult issue for both group members and facilitator alike. Silence can be interpreted in many different ways depending on the context within which it arises; some forms may indicate positive and helpful behaviour, while others may suggest problems and difficulties.

Silence within the group might, for example, indicate that learners are reflectively thinking about an issue, or concentrating on the task in hand. We have noted elsewhere that groups which are 'bubbling' are not necessarily groups that are learning. On the opposite side of this coin, groups that are silent are not necessarily doing nothing. This kind of silence can be reflective, constructive and worthwhile for learning, particularly if it leads to disclosure.

Given other supporting indicators, however, a learner's silence might suggest shyness or embarrassment, withdrawal or avoidance. Alternatively, it might indicate non-cooperation or resistance. It can require skill and even a little questioning to correctly interpret the reason for silence, to allow you to address it effectively and to get individual and group learning back on track. Whatever the motivating causes, silence frustrates the learning process by presenting a very real barrier to effective involvement and disclosure; if it is not addressed, opportunities for the learner to add issues of personal importance and relevance to the learning agenda will be lost.

Strategies for dealing with silence

- At the group level, describe the behaviour you are observing, confront the issue, eg, *'People aren't saying much at the moment and this is slowing things down. Is there a problem?'*
- Confront the issue at the individual level, eg, *'Susan, you made some interesting and useful points earlier but you now seem quieter, is this a difficult area for you?'*, or, *'I'd be interested to hear your views on this issue, John'.*
- Use encouraging non-verbal communication.
- Try using closed questions to get people to open up, eg, *'Do you agree with what's been said about listening skills, Matt?'*
- Use silence yourself, provided it is coupled with supportive and encouraging non-verbal communication.
- Use safe or less demanding exercises or learning activities to encourage learners to open up.

Cynicism

> *'A lot of the stuff that people are saying in this group is idealistic nonsense, there's a great deal of talk about understanding each person's point of view and taking it into account when you try and resolve a dispute, but in a real situation those things simply don't work and you end up shouting and arguing along with the "best" of them'.*

This disclosure was made by a group member during one of several facilitated sessions which sought to encourage learners to think about and identify various interpersonal skills involved in successful dispute resolution. To capture the problems created by this behaviour it's necessary to understand the dismissive, 'I-know-better-than-you' way in which it was said. Perhaps the learner had ventured to try out some of the strategies he was disparaging and had found them unworkable; perhaps not. Certainly his cynical viewpoint suggested he had difficulty accepting the ideas and suggestions offered on the course. This was a disclosure in itself, and a good starting point from which to work through the implications of what had been said.

Cynicism such as this must be unpacked and its various causes and implications considered, interpreted and discussed. Such remarks openly question the validity of the group's work, albeit in a denigrating fashion. It may be that there is a degree of accuracy inherent in the argument, and this can usefully be exposed by the very process of taking seriously remarks that are often intended as throwaway comments. If learners see that they are unable to upset the momentum of the course in this way, and that disparaging and cynical remarks are taken up and their consequences considered, they will be less inclined to say things they would rather not have discussed openly and seriously by the group.

Strategies for dealing with cynicism

- Let the learners vent their feelings and dump them in the group. The group might well deal with the cynicism itself.
- Take any cynical remark as a contribution, ask for clarification and work through its consequences openly. If there is any truth in what has been said, admit it and use it.
- Thank the learner for their contribution, perhaps remarking on the manner that it was offered to the group.
- Respond to cynical views with facts or information. This is particularly useful in fair treatment training where the attitude is based on common misconceptions about, say, minority groups. Pre-course information to dispose of expected 'old chestnuts' may be of great help in this respect.
- Stay calm, even if takes an effort. That way, if the purpose of the cynical behaviour is to produce an effect on you the facilitator, you will be able to show that you are really in control of the situation.
- Encourage the learner to consider a broader view of the issue which is generating the cynicism.

Interruptions and shutting out

To enable learners to have the opportunity and space to make effective contributions to the group, it may often become necessary for the facilitator to exert control over the flow of the discussion, thus ensuring that each group member has a fair chance to speak and become involved in the discussion. The more lively and responsive the group becomes, the more likelihood there is for difficult and problematic behaviour to arise in the form of over-talking, interruptions and shutting-out. As learners can clearly see the immediate and direct relevance and usefulness of training that is facilitated within a real-world framework, their enthusiasm, commitment and energy increase, and with it their involvement and contributions at all levels. As such, the real world facilitator must become more aware than most of the effects of poor communication skills within the training setting, and the way that such difficult behaviour creates barriers to open and effective involvement.

Strategies for dealing with interruptions and shutting out

- At the outset of any course discuss the problems posed by interruptions, over-talking and shutting-out and encourage learners to monitor their own behaviour in this regard.
- Acknowledge the interruptions and offer to get back to the person at a more appropriate moment.
- Control the interruption by enforcing a stronger discipline within the group as a whole. You may need to suggest to the group that the process is being impeded by people not giving each other space to speak without interruption.
- Take time out from any discussion to remind the group of the need to balance contributions with the need to listen and understand the contributions of others.
- Put the problem of poor communication skills into a real-world context as a way of illustrating its consequences for learners in day-to-day situations.
- Use your own non-verbal communication such as facial expression, hand gestures, or body position to shut off persistent interruptions.
- Balance the needs of the group by exercising your judgement about the need for individuals to get their point across without trespassing on the rights of others to have their say. This really is a key factor in facilitation where you, as the facilitator, have the responsibility to watch for the signs and take control of the discussion.

Avoidance

The problem of learner avoidance and possible strategies for addressing it were discussed in detail in Chapter 6.

Non-relevant contributions

Where a learner makes a contribution to the group or asks a question, neither of which are directly relevant to the issue being focused on, and this is done in a conscious effort to steer the conversation away from an area which is challenging and demanding for the learner, the behaviour amounts to a form of avoidance, and can be addressed as such. Conversely, where a learner introduces a red herring for non-directive reasons, there may be several explanations. The most likely one we have experienced is that the individual involved is simply not following the flow of the discussion and doesn't realize that the comment is not directly relevant.

As with other forms of avoidance, the potential problems posed in these circumstances can amount to an unnecessary shift of the group's attention away from the issues in hand; this is so even if the contribution was not made intentionally with this in mind. It should be remembered that any learner will, from time to time, make a contribution which misses the point, as they grapple with their own reactions to what is being discussed. In such circumstances the facilitator should allow the learner space to interpret their own contributions in light of the main topic, offering guiding questions to bring their discussion back on track.

Strategies for dealing with non-relevant contributions

- Re-focus the group
- Summarize the learning up to that point in the particular learning phase.
- Select an exercise or learning event which will help the group to get back on course.
- Co-facilitate with a partner who may have thought of an alternative way of dealing with the problem.
- Remind the group of the stated aim and learning intentions of the session.
- Briefly work with the learner to try to establish the relevance of what they have said.
- Keep the facilitation anchored in the real world of your learners and they will be less inclined to introduce red herrings.

Anger

During the course of an effective training session in which the issues discussed are important and significant to the learner, emotions can and often do run high. On occasions these feelings may include open anger directed at the topic, the group, a specific group member, or the facilitator. As with all forms of difficult behaviour, it is crucial that you take care to capture the exact size and shape of the behaviour and interpret it accurately *before* moving on to address it with the individual.

In the case of anger it is important to grasp why the emotion has arisen and at whom it is directed. It is also necessary to correctly interpret whether the anger can be positively harnessed and transformed into learning, or whether it is destructive, requiring a different approach. Examples of the former might include:

- Where a learner becomes angry at the injustice suffered by a minority group as the result of prejudice.
- Where a learner becomes angry at members of the group for their resistance to or avoidance of important issues under discussion.

Examples of the latter might involve:

- A learner becoming angry, believing it to be an appropriate alternative to involvement and disclosure.
- Anger resulting from a heated argument within the group, which the facilitator has failed to manage effectively.

Strategies for dealing with anger

- Stay calm, get *yourself* under control and don't take it personally. This is important, because in your role as facilitator, people will look to you to deal with the anger, and other members of the group will take advantage of not being personally responsible. (You may have been a learner in a group when something has happened that you were glad you did not have to deal with.)
- Don't get involved yourself. Keep thinking.
- Try to identify the source and direction of the anger, understand its meaning.
- Work through the reasons why the person feels as they do. Do they need information or support; are they frustrated?
- Diffuse the anger by identifying and dealing with the source.
- Reflect back to the learner that you understand that he or she is angry, or, if you suspect that a person is feeling angry, say what you see and check if you are right. If you are, at least you will then know what you are dealing with.
- Try to empathize.
- Find out if other people are feeling the same – help to spread the load.
- Work through the consequences of the anger with the learner and the group, placing such behaviour in a real-world context where possible.

Intolerance

When learners enter the training environment they may well be asked to manage their own behaviour in accordance with rules that they are not used to following in their own real world. It may be that involvement in group discussion and other forms of group activity represent new experiences for them and initially, without direct experience to call upon, they may attempt to resolve any frustrations they feel or interpersonal problem they face by calling upon recipes for action which do not fit well in the training setting.

By far the most common instance of this is intolerance of others within a group setting which often shows itself non-verbally through behaviour such as smirking, rolling of the eyes, shaking of the head, tutting, etc.

Strategies for dealing with intolerance

- Encourage the learner to have a raised awareness of the behaviour they are exhibiting, and its consequences.
- Tell the learner what you are seeing and hearing and what messages you are picking up – make them aware of how they are coming across to you. *'Brad, I notice that every time someone in the group says the word "gays" you shake your head and sigh, and it makes me think you have a different view on this issue'*.
- Identify the consequences of intolerance with the individual and the whole group.

Non-involvement

Facilitated learning is sometimes a new and threatening experience for some people, one which, when faced with the reality, proves to be too much for them. The result can be non-involvement, brought about through timidity and shyness. Unlike avoidance, it is not the challenging nature of the issues which motivates this withdrawal, but the risk of the unknown. Such reserve and lack of confidence obviously creates a barrier to involvement for the individual, which must be overcome if significant learning is to be achieved.

Strategies for dealing with non-involvement

- Where possible, introduce learner involvement at a safe, less challenging level initially, allowing learners to grow in confidence as they try out each new exercise or learning activity.
- Speak to the person during an interval and reassure them that they are valued members of the group and that they will learn best by joining in with the learning activities and discussion.
- Try placing the learner in a very small group learning activity.
- Ask each member of the group for their thoughts, by doing a round-robin type of feedback, where each member has to speak. In the early stages you would need to restrict what was being asked for to something quite bland and non-threatening.
- Pair the person with an energetic partner or even a co-facilitator. This may have the desired effect of energizing the person a little, but may of course make them feel even less confident.
- Pair the person with another timid member. You can try this if you have identified more than one non-participant.
- Describe to the learner what you see. Gently ask for an explanation of what you are observing.

FACILITATOR VULNERABILITY

We cannot leave the subject of difficult behaviour without considering the issue of facilitator vulnerability. Take a few moments to glance back at the pause for thought on page 132. If you haven't taken the opportunity to think about a training situation in which you were glad you were a learner and not the facilitator, then do it now. There is a strong probability that your own vulnerability comes in to the equation somewhere. None of us particularly relishes the idea of dealing with an angry group member, for example, or having to deal with a cynical or bad-mannered learner. Such aspects of a facilitator's role are often demanding and seldom easy.

Here are some suggestions to minimize your own vulnerability:

- Be aware of your own strengths and weaknesses and work within your own limits. Trying out new and challenging ways of working with learning groups can leave you vulnerable, and this in turn can threaten both your own development and the consequent learning of your group members. Try new methods in the safest environment possible, developing your skills gradually.

- Try to become aware of your own prejudices and capacity to stereotype, thinking through how they can impact on the ways you think and act with learners. The behaviours you find most difficulty in resolving may well link into your own attitudes, values and opinions.

- Acknowledge your own contributions (if any) to the difficult behaviour displayed. Has the way you dealt with the learner or the group added in some way to the resulting problem? Self-reflection is a fundamental aspect of your personal development as facilitator and where difficulties arise you should always attempt to establish the way in which you behaved, and the manner in which you chose to facilitate at the time.

- Confront your own fears. You will be expecting your learners to confront issues which they find challenging and difficult; if you believe that facing up to issues is a means of personal development for the learner, it follows that you too will benefit from facing up to what you fear most about facilitation. Treat your fears as opportunities to develop, rather than hurdles which you cannot jump.

- Keep your facilitation real-world. This means taking note of the Real-world Facilitation principles described in this book which are, we believe, fundamental to the success of this type of work. You will become vulnerable to a range of difficult behaviours arising from learner frustration, impatience, apathy, or dismissive attitude, if you don't work towards maximizing the relevance, significance and usefulness of learning.

- Don't pretend to be neutral about the content of your work if you are not. You will not be able to prevent leakage of your own views and if you try to pretend otherwise the group will find your deception to be a difficult behaviour in itself. To avoid becoming drawn into arguments between individuals is not the same thing as staying neutral, a position which, in any event, is difficult to sustain in the real world, and moreover is an unacceptable position when you are dealing with issues of fairness or equality.

- Be aware of your own position within the power structure. There are several ways in which this may have a bearing on your own vulnerability. If, for example, you are facilitating a peer group they may well spend a lot of energy in looking for inconsistencies in what you normally do, in the real world, and what you are saying as the facilitator of their learning. If the group consists in whole or in part of people who are normally in authority over you, it may take a while to establish the rules under which you can all comfortably work together. It will certainly need you to be confident in what you are doing.

- Keep your own expectations and personal objectives rooted in the real world of what is achievable. If you have diligently planned and prepared for a training session, it is not unreasonable to have high expectations of what might be achieved. In our experience, however, learners rarely have 'Damascus Road' experiences where they suddenly have a heavenly revelation of where they have been going wrong. Small steps towards meaningful, significant and relevant learning are much more likely.

- Don't take on exceptionally difficult content before you have tried your skills out in other less challenging areas. We have found that equal opportunities and fair treatment training is the hardest to tackle, because it tends to unearth deep-seated attitudes, opinions, beliefs and prejudices which can create highly charged atmospheres in which you need to feel confident of your ability to cope. We would not recommend tackling such topics unless you have first tried work in other areas, such as quality of service, assertiveness, team-building, self awareness and communication.

CHAPTER 8

Facilitating with Another Person

Outline

Up to this point we have assumed that you will be the one responsible for planning, delivering and reflecting upon the training that you undertake. It is not uncommon, however, for facilitators to work together at some or all stages of the facilitative process; we ourselves have often done so. In this chapter, we begin by considering the arguments both for and against working with a colleague. Effective co-facilitation needs communication, agreement and demarcation. We consider these important issues, as well as the support and feedback which can spring from working together. Such a joint training structure may produce significantly different effects on the group dynamic from those experienced by a facilitator working alone. We will also identify some of these differences. The chapter also includes practical suggestions for visual methods of recording the learning process as the course develops, and concludes with a consideration of the effects of co-facilitation on the learning group.

Planned learning outcomes

After you have read through this chapter we anticipate that you will:

- Have a better understanding of the arguments both for and against facilitating with another person.

- *Have thought through some of the issues surrounding working together with another facilitator.*
- *Have a better understanding of possible group reactions to your co-facilitation.*
- *Appreciate some of the practical issues associated with 'recording'.*

While there are many potential benefits in having two facilitators working together during a training session, the cost of providing this facility may well outweigh its advantages. This fact makes it doubly important that where there are opportunities to secure the expertise of two facilitators for one course, this co-facilitation must successfully enhance the effectiveness of the learning that results.

There are many issues that are unique to co-facilitation. Some of these issues centre upon the positive effects it can have on student learning, some on the skills necessary to realize these positive outcomes, while others address the potential problems that may arise when two facilitators act jointly to encourage learning with a single group of learners.

Pause for Thought

From your own experience, whether as a facilitator or as a learner on a facilitated training course:

- *Can you identify some of the potential benefits of co-facilitation, for both you and the learning group?*
- *Can you identify some of the potential pitfalls and problems?*

ARGUMENTS IN FAVOUR OF CO-FACILITATION

Sharing the work

If you are already facilitating, or intend to, you will know how much work it involves. At the end of a day's session, particularly with a group that has demonstrated high energy levels, it is not uncommon to feel physically, mentally and emotionally drained. The assistance of another facilitator can help to alleviate this, and such benefits are not restricted to the delivery phase;

the systematic planning and preparation required in Real-world Facilitation can also benefit from two people working in concert.

Sharing the stress

Picking up on the point of feeling emotionally drained at the end of a session, it is true to say that facilitation can be stressful for a number of reasons, such as the demanding nature of the content of your training course, the behaviour of the group you are working with (which may be challenging or difficult), and how you are actually feeling on the day. Having another person to share the responsibility and workload can effectively reduce this stress. On the many occasions we have worked together, we have been able to vent our feelings on each other, whether they be anger, confusion or satisfaction, and have felt better for it.

Addressing difficult individual or group behaviour can also be a very challenging and demanding part of the facilitator's work, often requiring him or her to suppress their own feelings and to remain objective, so as not to become embroiled in argument. Co-facilitators can offer each other mutual support at such times, thereby limiting the stress that such situations can cause.

Sharing perceptions

In earlier chapters on avoidance and difficult behaviour, we discussed the importance of constantly monitoring what is happening in the group, by watching, listening and interpreting the verbal and non-verbal messages of learners. This process can become more effective and more accurate if two facilitators are involved, as, whether we like to admit it or not, most of us stereotype or misinterpret behaviour from time to time.

We were working on a course together and anticipated some resistance to the training that we would undertake. Having arrived early at the course-room, we set everything up and, as usual, were greeting people as they arrived. One individual entered the room, took one look at us, ignored our greeting, and sat down and read his morning paper. I was convinced that his behaviour was going to prove difficult for me, although during the opening phase of the course he gave no real sign either way.

At the first interval, as so often happens, we discussed our initial impressions of the group. I asked my colleague if he had seen this learner ignore our greeting at the beginning. He hadn't, and as a result, had been looking at the person in a different light throughout the opening session, seeing him as both interested and helpful. As

145

the day progressed it became apparent that he was shy, but of all
the people there, was possibly the most committed to achieving
significant learning on the course.

This example demonstrates that it is helpful to check out initial impressions and to test them for validity and accuracy *before* acting on them.

Monitoring verbal and non-verbal behaviour and remaining alert to how people are reacting to the learning process, and to each other, is a vital part of the trainer's role within Real-world Facilitation. Two sets of eyes and ears can prove to be a real advantage, particularly where the group is relatively large and it is physically quite difficult to monitor all of the learners all of the time. Make use of these shared perceptions, discussing them and interpreting and validating their meaning and consequences as a joint process.

Being a sounding board

During the planning phase of any facilitated course, there is a need to design in flexibility, enabling learners to determine parts of the course agenda for themselves, thus ensuring that resultant learning is kept directly relevant and meaningful to them. One consequence of this requirement is that you must also remain flexible at the point of course delivery, being prepared to introduce an exercise or learning activity which was not part of your original facilitative plan. In such circumstances, it is often a good idea to discuss these 'mid-course corrections' with your colleague, who may be able to suggest an alternative way forward or confirm your ideas as being worth trying. Act as a sounding board for each other, by exchanging ideas and observations at every available opportunity. In this way you will be making the most of your combined expertise and experience.

Changing style and pace

Much of what we have said so far focuses on you, the facilitator. But given that the advantages discussed should result in improved group and individual learning, it follows that learners can also gain from co-facilitated training. In summary these benefits might include:

- A change of face. It can be very refreshing for a group to have a different person leading it, and the longer the course is, the more important this may become. Boredom can set in if the same facilitator is there hour after hour – unfortunately, we are rarely as interesting and lively as we like to think we are!
- A change of pace. Group energy levels can rise and fall as the result of a

number of factors which were discussed in Chapter 3. Injecting a change of pace can either raise or suppress energy as necessary, and this can be achieved by allowing another person to take the lead.

- A change of style. There is a rich variety of possible styles of facilitation, and we each have a different profile of skill, ability and interest. Switching the leadership of the group and thus the style of facilitation it receives, can be refreshing for learners, some of whom might be better adapted to certain learning styles than others.

- A change of emphasis. No two facilitators work in quite the same way, and can often explore issues by placing emphasis on different aspects of the subject being discussed. This change of emphasis can serve to invigorate the group.

- Being able to split the group up. A significant benefit inherent in co-facilitation is the opportunity to split the learning group in two and to work with each half as a separate unit. Such arrangements can allow methods of facilitation not usually possible, for example:

  - each group can follow a different aspect of the learning agenda for part of the course
  - learners may enjoy wider choice as to the direction they wish their training to take
  - exercises and learning activities can be speeded up as a consequence of being able to prepare separate groups at the same time – role players and observers, for example
  - you will be able to monitor small group work more closely
  - you can improve the learner/trainer ratio by facilitating smaller groups
  - you will be in a position to provide individual support to learners when they need it, allowing one facilitator to counsel a person in need while the other continues to work with the group.

Although any or all of these advantages are possible, you should be careful not to upset the continuity and cohesion of the learning process. This can happen if one half of the group is allowed to move forward at a faster pace than the other, or move off in a completely different direction. There is also the danger that lack of time may not allow learners to cover those parts of the learning agenda that they have missed as a result of these facilitative arrangements.

These pitfalls can be avoided if you work to ensure that dividing your resources in this way serves to complement your overall training plan. Nevertheless, you should keep in close contact throughout and remain aware of the problems that might arise.

ARGUMENTS AGAINST CO-FACILITATION

Before discussing the arguments against co-facilitation, it is worth noting that, in the real world, there is sometimes little if any choice in such matters. We have twice been in the situation where the number of facilitators working with a group was a matter of policy, made on the basis of advice from an outside consultant.

Disagreement

It can become difficult to facilitate with a colleague when you have significant disagreement over aspects of the facilitative process.

In terms of the content of your training course, you need to agree the agenda you will be working through. For example, do you both accept that the suggested topics are the most important and significant for your learners? Is the course properly structured? Do you share an understanding of the topics you will be covering, their implications and application?

In terms of process, you will need to reach agreement concerning your choice and use of exercises and learning activities, while also agreeing that you will not insist on a rigid adherence to your plan, should flexibility be required to enhance the relevance, significance and usefulness of the learning.

Conflict of style and personality

We noted above that two possible advantages of co-facilitation are that it offers the group a change of face and a change of pace and therefore helps to keep up energy levels. Where styles conflict, however, this contrast can work against the promotion of effective learning to the extent that it would be better not to co-facilitate at all. For example, this might occur when one of the facilitators is more authoritarian (control-centred) than the other, or has a more didactic, directing style. Alternatively, a strong, more extrovert facilitator might overshadow a more introverted colleague, whose strengths might not be so visible. While we would live in a poorer world if we all had the same personality, where there is a wide disparity it can lead to co-facilitative problems.

Lack of empathy

A lack of empathy between co-facilitators can also frustrate the learning process. To work together effectively requires both trainers to have an awareness and an understanding of each other's styles, skill and needs, and the ability to anticipate and interpret what is going on between a facilitator and a learning group at any given time.

> *On a one-day seminar dealing with issues of quality of service, two facilitators were working together. They had not met before and therefore had little, if any, empathy for or understanding of each other's style and approach. At one point the facilitator leading the group asked a very penetrating question resulting in a long period of silence, which he decided to run with in order to allow learners space to reflect. The other facilitator had no understanding of what was going on and assumed that his colleague needed rescuing from what he perceived to be a destructive and embarrassing silence. He chimed in and said, 'Well if no one's going to say anything we might as well all go home'. The first facilitator cringed, knowing that the learning atmosphere that he had worked so hard to engender had been destroyed.*

Lack of commitment

Where the commitment to address challenging issues is not shared by both facilitators, friction can arise. It can appear as if one facilitator is doing all the difficult, confronting and challenging work, picking up on issues as they surface, while the other has a relatively easy time of it, not becoming involved in demanding situations, allowing avoidance to go unchallenged, and failing to offer any significant personal disclosure.

This can prove frustrating for the facilitator who is committed to confronting and addressing real-world issues, problems and experiences, but who is forced to sit on the sidelines during his or her colleague's sessions, while such learning opportunities are inadequately dealt with. Such frustration can be increasingly fuelled by a colleague who persistently fails to challenge issues of fairness. Statements which are racist, sexist, or in some other way problematic should not be left to pass unchallenged. It can be intensely frustrating to witness the loss of excellent learning opportunities and to stand by while a colleague allows this to happen.

Conflicting messages

If not dealt with, the potential problems of co-facilitation we have outlined in this section can lead to the learning group receiving inconsistent or even conflicting messages about the relative importance of the issues being discussed, and how best to address them. Learners are rarely blind to such conflicts, or immune to their effects on learning.

Summary of the arguments

Although there are many arguments both for and against co-facilitation, if there is one overriding lesson we have learned from working together, it is the need to be *totally honest* with each other; but how will this work out in practice?

- It means that you will need to know each other before you work together.
- It means that you will need to have reached agreement concerning your facilitative strategy. Are you both committed to Real-world Facilitation principles for example?
- It means that if you disagree at the planning stage then you must say so, and must work together to clarify and address areas of conflict before they are allowed to undermine your training plan at the point of course delivery.
- It means that you must arrive at a consensus regarding demarcation. Who is to facilitate which learning phases, and how will you change over?
- It means that you must agree on and adhere to your own ground rules as you facilitate. For example, if you agree to remain silent while your colleague is facilitating, then stay silent.
- It means that when your colleague asks for feedback on how it is going, you give an honest reply and, in turn, you give permission for your partner to be honest about *your* performance without becoming defensive.
- Taken together, these arguments can mean that you will present a more consistent and coherent overall message to your learners, and the group is less likely to be put off track by conflicts in your approach.

Figure 8.1 gives a quick summary of some of the positive and negative aspects of co-facilitation.

RECORDING

Up to this point we have spoken primarily about co-facilitation. This assumes that both facilitators work side-by-side, encouraging learning together. One very common way of co-facilitating however, is for one person to actually facilitate, while the other acts as a 'recorder'. Recording usually means keeping records of the learning process by noting relevant and significant aspects of the group's activities and discussions, and displaying these on A1 size 'flipchart' paper (also called 'newsprint'). As sheets become filled, they can be taped to the walls of the course room. This written work provides the group with a permanent record of what has taken place and how the course has developed.

Potential for:-

Change of style,
pace and emphasis

Sharing the work

Sharing perceptions

Sharing the stress

Being a sounding
board

Potential for:-

Disagreements

Conflict of interes
style or personalit

Lack of empathy

Lack of commitm

Sharing the glory

Conflicting mess;

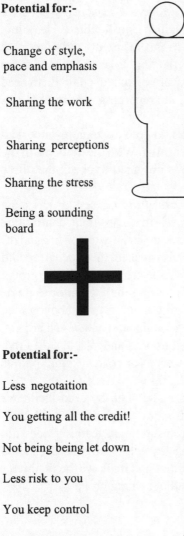

Potential for:-

Less negotaition

You getting all the credit!

Not being being let down

Less risk to you

You keep control

Potential for:-

Stress

Bored group

No support or fee

Being tired

Figure 8.1   *The positives and negatives of co-facilitation*

151

Recording performs several very useful functions in terms of Real-world Facilitation; these can be usefully summarized as follows.

- Most people who attend meetings are used to having minutes taken; they form a useful record of what was said and by whom. The opportunity to refer back to what has taken place, and to have a reasonably accurate record of what was said, can also be invaluable in facilitated learning. Discussions can often be wide-ranging, needing key points and significant issues drawn off and recorded for later reflection. Likewise, agendas are often developmental and built in stages; ideas contained within them need to be reduced into workable issues, and good recording can simplify this important task.

- Real-world Facilitation constantly seeks to maximize relevance and meaning, thereby unlocking significant learning. With the thoughts of the group being recorded, a ready reference is provided to check that these fundamental themes are being kept centre-stage.

  A good example of this is where a group 'brainstorming' session has taken place. The central feature of any brainstorm is that everything contributed by the group should be included. Comments are usually quick-fire and off the top of the head. When the brainstorm has finished, the flipchart record of the session should be full of ideas that have been generated by the group. At this stage, learners can relax a little, allowing the facilitator to guide them through their work, before encouraging them to think about which ideas are relevant and useful to the discussion in hand and which are not. By categorizing and linking their contributions, and placing different learning values on them, the group will start to impose meaning on this information, a key process in real-world learning.

- It is more effective if such recording is undertaken by a co-facilitator (where one is available), as it provides structure to the working relationship that exists between each trainer. It ensures that learning does not become lost. It overcomes the need to use a learner – who should really be participating and contributing – as a recorder, and it allows the facilitator to focus all his attention on working with the learning group.

Recording also has its pitfalls however.

- *Its purpose needs to be clearly explained.* Although we have mentioned the value of keeping minutes in an example above, there may be some learners who are not used to having notes taken of what they say. This can lead to suspicion and unease. Accordingly, the need, extent and usefulness of recording should be openly discussed with learners at the outset. Advantages that can be raised with them include the following suggestions:

- it will help people's views to be represented fairly
- it will chart the progress of the group through the agenda
- it will help later reflection as the course progresses
- it will provide a written record of what has been said and what ideas have been generated.

Learners will also need to know what will happen to the material after the session, and if you agree that it should be destroyed, then make sure that this happens, in the presence of the group if necessary. Alternatively, there are very real benefits to be gained from transferring flipchart notation to a more permanent and accessible record of the course, providing learners with material which will help them with the process of post-course reflection. A potential barrier to transferring learning from a training to a real-world setting is that learners quickly forget the good ideas and strategies generated on a course. The provision of a well structured and usable summary of key learning points will help to overcome this barrier.

- *It can lose credibility if not done accurately.* Having discussed the value of recording with the group, it must then be done properly if it is to retain credibility.

    On occasions we have seen recorders write things that quite clearly did not reflect the learner's statement. As soon as the learner realized that they were being misrepresented, they angrily rounded on the facilitator demanding to know what was going on, believing that they were being set up in some way.

There are three specific factors to remember to ensure accurate recording. First, listen carefully to what is being said. Second, where possible, use the words spoken and not an interpretation or translation of them. Third, don't rush the process; stop to ask for clarification if necessary. If there is some doubt, encourage learner involvement by asking such questions as 'What would *you* like put up?', or, 'How would you like this worded?' In this way, contributions remain the property of the speaker, and will carry that much more authority and credibility for both the individual and the group.

- *Terms have to be used with care.* It is all too easy to slip into 'facilitator speak' and, almost unconsciously, to convert what is being said into either facilitation-like terminology, or words which express what you have in mind for the content and process, rather than what is actually happening.

Some examples of what we have heard learners saying, and what has actually been recorded, before being challenged, include:

153

'I have difficulty liking gay people' = homophobia
'They've all got a chip on their shoulder' = prejudice
'There are certain jobs that men are simply better at than women'
= stereotyping.

The point about these summarizing labels isn't that they are necessarily inaccurate, but that they superimpose the facilitator's (or recorder's) interpretation of what the learner's contribution means. Don't pre-empt the learning that group members will gain from working through the meaning of such contributions themselves. They may feel less comfortable with the labelling of attitudes in such a blanket fashion.

We have seen other examples of things recorded which are less than helpful to most groups.

A page drawn up by one recorder, resulting from group-work where the learners had been working in groups of three, was headed: 'Triadic feedback'. Some members of the group thought this referred to a Chinese secret society!

To be effective, the contents of written material must be meaningful to your learners, and this is best achieved by using terms, phrases and words that they readily understand and tend to use themselves in everyday situations.

- *It needs to be readable and interesting.* Recording is of little value if it cannot be read easily. This means that you should pay attention to the size and readability of your writing. Try to use a style with no frills, and avoid the overuse of capital letters as far as possible. In general, capital letters are used in written English or American language to signify names, or the beginning of a sentence. When these rules are broken, readability is reduced.

Where a number of separate issues are recorded, it is useful to identify the paragraph, sentence or word by putting some sort of symbol beside it, often termed a 'bullet' (as we have tended to do with lists in this book) and then indenting from the left margin. You can be creative in your design of bullet and this will help to make written records more interesting and more accessible. Another way of brightening up your recording is to use colour to signify themes, issues or categories. Remember the implied messages of red and green (stop and go, danger and safety and so on) and be careful not to place a value on some material by an unconscious choice of colour.

- *Some hints on recording (see Figure 8.2)*

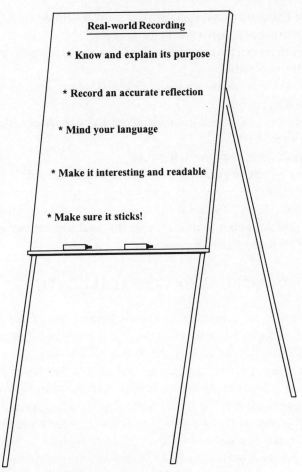

Figure 8.2 *Things to think about when recording*

- Explain the recording process to the group in a clear and straightforward way, highlighting the benefits.
- Ensure learners realize that they can question the accuracy and meaning of things that have been recorded.
- Always make sure that what has been recorded accurately reflects what has been said.
- Check with learners any contributions which seem unclear or difficult to summarize.
- If a contribution seems to lack relevance to issues under discussion, say so to the group.
- Use everyday terms, phrases and words.

- Don't superimpose your own interpretation of the meanings of learner contributions; leave this to the group.
- Try to record the exact words and phrases used by the person contributing if possible.
- Ensure that handwriting is legible and is large enough to be read with ease by all.
- Don't put too much information on any one sheet and number pages as appropriate.
- Don't write in capital letters only.
- Use bullets or dashes to make paragraphs and points stand out from each other.
- Leave plenty of space for later additions and amendments.
- If you are going to put work on the wall, use temporary tape which will not damage wall coverings.

ACTUALLY CO-FACILITATING

So far then, we have considered the arguments both for and against co-facilitation, and have suggested that the role of recorder might be a useful one to undertake when not actually in the 'hot seat'. We strongly recommend that you do not actually facilitate *together,* in the sense that you share the leading of a discussion or share the responsibility of guiding the group through the process at a given point. We do recommend that when you take on the role of recorder, you stay with it and do not interfere with the facilitative process at all, unless invited to do so by the facilitator, or there is a need to clarify contributions for recording purposes. In this way the recorder can focus on that task, listening, being accurate and making the recorded material interesting, accessible and readable, while at the same time supporting the person actually facilitating, by monitoring verbal and non-verbal messages and behaviour. As the recorder, these tasks will keep you fully occupied while leaving the facilitator free to concentrate on working with the learning group. Your training plan should cater for regular reversal of these two roles, and you can always suggest a change if either of you feels the need for a break, or you feel that you could steer the group more effectively with a different approach. If you are being honest with each other you will not be afraid to suggest this.

Working together effectively requires that you consider and address four important aspects of co-facilitation: managing disagreement, coordinating demarcation, effective in-course communication and feedback. We have chosen to deal with these issues in pairs as they tend to occur together naturally.

Agreement and demarcation

If you plan to co-facilitate a training session, then issues of agreement and demarcation should ideally be discussed openly and honestly at the outset, ie, when you are planning and preparing course content and process. Here, issues of personal style, individual ability and preferences can be usefully identified, their consequences for learning and group dynamics considered, and workable and achievable co-facilitation strategies developed. This degree of joint forward planning will help both facilitators to feel comfortable with the overall training plan.

Most facilitated training is structured in a developmental way, ensuring that each learning phase builds naturally upon, and expands, a previous learning phase, while also providing a good basis from which to move on to the next. The boundaries between such phases are not always obvious and at times this may create difficulties of demarcation. Both of you may want to run with a particular learning phase, and this can frustrate attempts to ensure that time spent facilitating the group is fairly and evenly divided. Once agreed, however, such demarcation should be recorded somewhere on the training plan itself, so that individual responsibility for particular facilitative phases, and the change over between each, are clearly and unambiguously shown.

While we acknowledge that these issues can prove difficult to resolve, time spent at the beginning identifying potential conflict and agreeing demarcation and division of facilitative labour is time well spent. By carrying out this pre-course planning, you will ensure that you both enter the course itself from a common standpoint, safe in the knowledge that (accepting the need for flexibility in your approach) you both feel happy with your training plan and understand which phases each of you are responsible for facilitating. In short, you will present the group with a positive, professional, unified image, that demonstrates the fact that you work well together, understand the issues, and are both going in the same direction.

In-course communication and feedback

We have already stressed the need for effective communication between co-facilitators and would now like to offer some practical suggestions as to how this might be achieved as the course progresses.

- You will already have a detailed plan of who is scheduled to do what and when, and the first thing that you can monitor is how well you are adhering to that plan. It is easy to forget that you have overrun your turn at the helm, for example, and a timely reminder from your partner is useful.
- As the course develops, it is important that you exchange feedback on how

effectively each of you is applying Real-world Facilitation principles during your work with the group. This ongoing process will help you to focus your efforts on maximizing the relevance, significance and meaning of each aspect of your training.

- Energy levels can often be better detected by a recorder or co-facilitator who is not actually taking the lead at the time. Indeed, the co-facilitator might be experiencing a fall in his own energy level in sympathy with the group, and this might be undetected by the facilitator, who is not always alert to it.

- The monitoring of difficult behaviour should be another area for effective communication between you. What is being noticed, heard and felt? Do you understand and interpret these messages in the same way? What do you both think might be the implications or consequences of such behaviour?

- Exchange views and perceptions as to how the course is actually going. Are you encouraging learning that meets planned learning outcomes? Is learning progressing at the right pace? Are energy levels right? etc. Every aspect of your work together will benefit from such discussion and joint reflection.

- The personal performance of each partner is another area which will need to be discussed. Give each other permission to offer honest and constructive feedback, reflecting on its validity before saying what you think.

- Monitor aspects of each other's behaviour such as use of language and disclosed opinions and attitudes. Inappropriate behaviour can be very destructive of credibility and may at times occur unwittingly. Providing each other with sensitive feedback will enable you both to address this problem, should it arise.

Support

The last aspect of co-facilitation which needs consideration is support. Facilitation can be demanding and sometimes isolating work, and will often drain you mentally and emotionally. You can use an enormous amount of energy during a day where you have had to remain constantly alert, thinking fast, adapting, and working at several levels, particularly on courses which prove demanding, or where members of the group have exhibited difficult behaviour.

In such circumstances, it can be very liberating to be able to share that stress with someone who, because they are working alongside you, will understand your experiences, and can extend mutual support. Let's face it, there will be times, as is so often the case in the real world, when you just want to have a good moan about what has happened.Alternatively, you may want to share the pleasure of having encouraged significant learning for your group. All these things are part of the shared experience of facilitators working together.

THE EFFECTS OF CO-FACILITATION ON THE LEARNING GROUP

We have facilitated groups individually and together, and our observations suggest that these different situations have very different effects on learning groups. The very fact that two facilitators are working together could signal that there is something special about the course. As we have said, in these times of limited resources, the luxury of co-facilitation may well be interpreted as overkill by learners. Typical responses might be:

- Is trouble expected?
- What has this course got in store for us?
- Is one of them (the facilitators) a learner?
- What a waste of resources.
- The money would be better spent on books (or whatever).
- Why do they need the backup, what's the problem?

Such feelings may never be expressed openly, but can nevertheless be very real for the group. The anxiety level of learners may be raised, or frustration may set in. It is important that you account for the possibility of such reactions from learners and address them at an early stage. A simple explanation may suffice, provided, of course, that *you* know why there are two of you working together.

We once experienced a problem in this respect. The sponsoring organization recognized that there might be resistance to the type of training we were about to undertake. Because the pool of facilitators available was inexperienced, many of them expressed the fear that they were not equal to the task. It was decided that the courses (which were to be of seven days' duration) would be facilitated by three trainers working together as a team. Each team would be required to run two courses, each separated by a month or two. Understandably, some of the facilitators felt uncomfortable with these arrangements, and expressed the view that there was no need to have more than two facilitators working with each group. The lack of cohesion which this caused was a problem for many of the groups at the outset. Overkill was obvious to the learners, who themselves were in fairly small groups. The strange situation arose

159

where three facilitators were confronting, almost literally, groups of ten learners. The obvious support apparent for the facilitators gave such a strong negative message to the learners, that it simply got in the way of their learning. Subsequently, some of the courses had to disband early in failure. This could have been for a number of reasons, but we remain convinced that such overkill was an important contributory factor.

There can of course be more positive reactions to co-facilitation such as:

- Whoever is sponsoring this training is really committed to the issues if they are prepared to make such an investment.
- These two people are obviously committed to the issues themselves.
- This is a good model of how teams can work together effectively.

In earlier chapters we have discussed how the facilitator's style, approach and personality all have a significant impact upon group dynamics. The way a learner feels about and works within the learning group is intricately inter-linked with the way his or her contributions are managed, the level of reward received, and the relationship that develops between him or herself and the facilitator.

Inevitably, on a co-facilitated training course, different group dynamics will develop as learners reflect on, and then react to, the relationship formed between the facilitators themselves and between each individual facilitator and members of the learning group.

Stay alert to this issue, and discuss with your partner both the positive and negative consequences of the group's reactions when one or other facilitator is leading the session. For example, if you sense that your widely differing approaches are having a negative effect on group dynamics, you might decide to try out ways of working together which minimize this reaction.

We have also found that if the degree of commitment shown to Real-world Facilitation varies greatly between co-facilitators, then the one who diligently seeks to lock on to the real-world issues, problems and experiences of the learners, will enjoy far greater credibility and facilitative success than the one who does not.

SUMMARY

In this chapter we have considered many of the issues surrounding co-facilitation from a real-world standpoint. We noted some of the arguments in favour of working together, and some of those against. The role of recorder was also discussed, and advice was offered as to how recording can enhance overall learning if done well. Factors involved in the process of co-facilitation at the point of both planning and course delivery were dealt with in some detail, and the need for effective communication between co-facilitators was emphasized. The chapter concluded with a consideration of the effects of co-facilitation on the learning group.

CHAPTER 9

Encouraging Future Action

Outline

Even though learners usually leave a training course with every intention of applying what they have learnt, all too often, and for many different reasons, the potential impact of training becomes diluted. In this final chapter we will explore some of the reasons for this and at the same time offer guidance on how to work with learners in ways that minimize barriers to future action or necessary change by the learner.

Planned learning outcomes

Having read this chapter we anticipate that you will have a better understanding of:

- *The potential barriers to applying learning to the learner's real world and ways of working with learners to minimize these.*
- *The importance of recording and saving learners' work throughout the training course.*
- *The need to summarize key learning, both as an ongoing process and as part of course closure.*
- *Ways of bringing courses to a close which encourage future action.*

Before taking a detailed look at barriers to applying learning in real-world contexts it will prove helpful to take another look at the future action principles, first described in Chapter 2 and set out again below.

FUTURE ACTION PRINCIPLES

These Real-world Facilitation principles relate to those parts of the course during which learners are encouraged to develop strategies for dealing with their own relevant issues and problems and to establish commitment to necessary future action.

- Strategies that you encourage group members to develop in response to their own problems, issues and experiences, should take account of:
  - the environment in which the strategy will ultimately be used
  - the power, or lack of it, of the learner in any given situation
  - any potential 'costs and benefits' to the learner of the chosen strategy
  - the skills required to put the strategy into practice
  - possible resistance to the strategy which they might discover within themselves or in others.
- Strategies that learners develop in order to deal with their own issues and problems should be realistic and achievable in the real world.
- You should attempt to maximize personal commitment on the part of the learner to put into practice those strategies developed on the course.
- In the real world, people need support. Try to generate realistic ideas about how the individual or group might seek out and use the support that is available.

The most likely reason for learners failing to transfer into the real world the learning achieved within the training setting is its *lack of fit with that reality*. Matters discussed with enthusiasm and commitment in the course room lose viability in the face of seemingly insurmountable problems posed by everyday situations. Strategies for dealing with 'this issue or that' seem naive and ineffectual, and new ways of looking at and thinking through problems ring hollow and lack bite. Real-world Facilitation has been developed from this very starting point, and demands an approach to training that systematically works through relevant, significant and meaningful problems and issues, before developing viable, useful and achievable responses. Nowhere is this more important than when encouraging learners to take that learning forward and to apply it where it really matters, in everyday problems and situations.

In the following section we discuss some of the barriers that confront those who are committed to transferring their learning from the training setting into the real world. As you consider each of them, it can be useful to remember that these barriers are intricately linked to the future action principles just described. If you are committed to the systematic application of these principles in your training, you will pre-empt the effects of such barriers by confronting and addressing their underlying causes.

BARRIERS TO THE APPLICATION OF LEARNING

Good training costs money, takes time, and is usually demanding of both facilitator and learner alike. Quite naturally, all those involved will want and expect to see a return on this investment. The facilitator will hope that he or she has been successful in encouraging and guiding the group to address the learning agenda and to achieve specific planned learning outcomes. The learner will hope to leave the course with a better understanding of existing issues and problems and ways of addressing and resolving them. The sponsor will hope that the course has enhanced the skills and abilities of participants, and has encouraged them to reflect upon the appropriateness of existing views and past behaviour and the need to change.

But the impact of learning achieved on any course is contingent upon its *application* to real-world issues and problems in real-world situations. Learning must be transferred from the training setting in which it was first identified and addressed, to the everyday contexts within which it arises and finds meaning. Movement from course-room to workplace requires the learner to cross the learning bridge and to put into practice the realistic and practical approaches to dealing with day-to-day situations and problems that were discussed as part of the learning agenda. Realistically however, many problems may beset learners in their efforts to transfer and apply to everyday occurrences the strategies and ideas learnt during training. Our own experience has shown that it is all too easy for the facilitator to ignore this important area, viewing barriers to the application of learning as somebody else's concern, believing that, as this problem arises after training, it is beyond his or her control.

This is an unfortunate assumption that must be addressed if facilitation is to be seen as an effective method of training which is capable of encouraging lasting learning and developing skills which prove useful in meeting real challenges. By tackling the obstacles which prevent the transference of problem-solving strategies and ideas into the real world of the learner, facilitators will provide their students with the best possible opportunity to adopt new skills and new ways of addressing real-world issues and problems.

It is important to remember that even though you may strive to make your training as real world as possible, there are many factors which separate any form of training from its application. Typically, people in training have gathered together for a common purpose that is of direct benefit to them, and this is often reflected in a high level of interest and commitment. The training setting is also a very controlled environment in which conflict or poor interpersonal skills are arbitrated by a skilled facilitator, who has a professional interest in the well-being and development of each learner. It is a safe environment in which (hopefully) individuals feel comfortable and able to disclose and exchange views and ideas, free from cynicism or attack. Many of these factors stand in marked contrast to the real world in which the learner lives and works.

Further, training is freed from the pressures and constraints of the real world, in which telephones constantly ring, people interrupt and deadlines loom. Facilitators, although managers of learning and group process, do not discipline or control in the same sense that line managers may. Also, by its very nature, training allows for mistakes and failure, for practice and development, whereas, in the real world, mistakes often have immediate consequences and there is little, if any, opportunity to try again.

The inherent difference between these two realities – that of the training setting and that of the learner's real world – while bridged, in part at least, by the real-world model itself, can create a false sense of ease and possibility within training which may lull both facilitator and learner alike into forgetting the problems and difficulties which impede the application of learning in the real world. What is needed is a more open and honest approach to the issues and challenges which separate these two realities, an approach that systematically confronts and seeks to address these problems head-on.

In the remainder of this chapter, we suggest several potential barriers, any one of which could frustrate the application of learning in a real-world setting. We then provide some suggested ways in which facilitators can work with learners to overcome them. Underpinning each of our strategies is the ongoing need to raise the issues and problems that are, or might be, associated with any suggested ways of dealing with problems and people, *as part of* any discussion of the viability and appropriateness of those suggestions.

Pause for Thought

From your own experience, either as a facilitator, or as a learner on a facilitated training course, can you:

- *Identify typical barriers to applying things learnt during training to everyday issues and problems?*
- *Suggest ways in which you might take account of such barriers as a trainer?*

Throughout this book we have emphasized the value and importance of drawing on the knowledge, skills and experiences of your learners, encouraging them to identify and explore the issues and problems that are significant for them. This holds true when considering methods of overcoming barriers to the transfer of learning into usable action and commitment to necessary change. After all, who knows better than the learner what potential pitfalls and hurdles are waiting to frustrate his or her best efforts?

Rather than waiting to the end of the course to raise these issues, we suggest that it is far more effective if they become an integral part of your work with the group. As you encourage learners to think about and discuss ways of addressing issues and problems, questions concerning their application should be asked.

BARRIERS TO APPLYING LEARNING – RAISED AND LOWERED

The Real-world Facilitation model requires that strategies, ideas, solutions and new ways of thinking and acting should be tested as they are raised (see Figure 9.1):

- Are they realistic?
- Can they be achieved?
- Are they useful and usable?
- Do they account for the realities of the situation or problem?

To these questions you can usefully add others which bear directly upon issues of resistance. Some suggestions include the following.

- *How does the learner feel about the prospect of tackling the issue or problem in the way suggested?*

There is a very real difference between agreeing about strategies and new ways

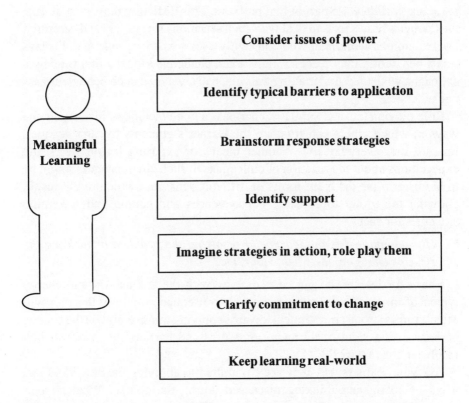

Figure 9.1 *Some ways to overcome barriers to transferring learning into action and necessary change*

of acting, in the safety of the training setting, and putting these ideas into practice in the real world, with its accompanying challenges and difficulties and the vulnerability this creates. Learners must be encouraged to think about these issues and to be honest and open if they feel that ideas being suggested by the group are overly ambitious or naive.

It can help if learners are allowed space to imagine themselves using such strategies or new ways of acting towards others, in real situations where colleagues have not had this training.

• *How might others feel about the learner tackling the issue or problem in the way suggested?*

Those who have not had the benefit of your training may resist or even resent a colleague who displays new skills, or tackles old problems in new ways, particularly if they are part of that problem. This difficulty may arise despite the learner's best efforts to deal with such situations sensitively and carefully. For example, a workmate who constantly uses sexist language and displays sexist behaviour, may react strongly when challenged for the first time by a colleague who, until undertaking training, had always let such behaviour pass unchallenged.

Role-playing this and similar scenarios is a good method of identifying the ways in which others can frustrate the learner's attempts to carry learning forward into everyday life. Another means of exposing learner fears and expectations about the reaction of colleagues in such circumstances might be to brainstorm the different forms of difficult behaviour which might result, allowing the group to consider consequences and coping and resolution strategies for each.

- *How committed is the learner to resolving the problem or tackling the issue or changing their behaviour, etc?*

It's easy for learners to get carried away with the enthusiasm and energy typical of an effective learning group. One consequence of this is that they will often express strong commitment towards applying things learnt on the course, perhaps losing sight of the many pressures and barriers that will test that resolve in the real world.

Ask your learners *why* they are committed to applying the new ideas and ways of acting and thinking discussed during the course. What is their motivation for carrying the learning forward? How will that commitment be tested in the weeks and months ahead? By clarifying their own reasons for applying new found skills, knowledge, attitudes and values, they will be identifying the source of their own commitment, a strength they can draw upon when that commitment is tested.

Using the Real-world Facilitation model, you will find that ideas, strategies and alternative ways of thinking and acting, suggested by group members, will have been formulated and developed as a direct response to existing issues, problems and experiences raised by the learners themselves. Accordingly, learners will be motivated to use this learning because it has immediate relevance and use. A systematic adherence to the dictates and principles of Real-world Facilitation will create a climate of credibility that will strengthen your learners' resolve to try out learning where it really matters – in the real world!

- *How might the learners' existing relationships interfere with their proposed action or change of behaviour?*

Most of us work in organizations which are hierarchies, structured with levels of management from top to bottom. Whether you are a supervisor or are yourself supervised, it is likely that your day-to-day relationships with others allow for the reality of power. This fact must not be overlooked in the training setting for, if future action and necessary change are to remain achievable and workable in a real-world setting, due regard must be given to each learner's ability to effect such change or undertake such action.

For example, if some form of organizational change is suggested by the group in order to address an important issue or resolve a problem, the process of change and its consequences must be thought through. Who will be affected by the change and how much resistance is likely to be encountered? Has due allowance been made for consultation with those affected? At what level must the proposed change be sanctioned? How will the support of senior managers be secured?

These are real-world considerations which must be tackled head-on if learning stands any chance of being applied. Failure to do so will almost inevitably lead to such proposed changes never becoming implemented, as learners, realizing the barriers they face and having no strategies for overcoming them, will place such issues and proposals in the 'too-hard tray'.

- *Will others accept personal change?*

Even though the courses that you run may only last a few days, if they are effective in encouraging and promoting learning, learners can undergo significant change. They may question and amend attitudes, begin the process of altering values and may leave the course with new ways of looking at, thinking about and dealing with both people and issues that are significant to them.

Two important factors can combine to disrupt this process of personal development after the learner has left the course and returned to the world of everyday life. It is likely that the learner will not be fully aware of changes that have taken place within himself, or of the different ways of behaving that may result. Because of this he or she will not be prepared for the reactions of others who know them and expect them to think and behave as before. Friends and colleagues in turn will find unexpected changes and may experience uncertainty as to how they should react to inconsistencies in the learner's behaviour, for he or she has moved on and they have not.

We have both experienced the real problems that this poses for all

169

concerned. Following an intense but rewarding course in counselling, and armed with fresh perspectives and a bag of new communication and facilitation skills, we returned home and afterwards to work. We soon discovered (although we didn't initially understand why) that our attempts to behave differently towards others and to express different views and opinions than before, unsettled and irritated colleagues and friends who were unprepared for these changes.

At first we interpreted their reactions as resistance to our new ideas and unnecessary conservatism. Later, and after several discussions, we realized that we had not prepared ourselves or others for this change in our behaviour and had not attempted to ease into these new ways of acting and thinking. In fact we had returned from the course equipped with almost missionary zeal and a lack of sensitivity as to the consequences.

- *Will other people's lack of skill frustrate the learner's intentions? Have they been taken into account?*

When learners are in the training setting working with other group members, they will be working alongside and exchanging views and ideas with others who have undertaken the same process as themselves. In addition, interpersonal problems and conflicts will be mediated by the facilitator, who will work to ensure learners communicate with each other in a sensitive and effective manner.

Both of these facilities are absent in the real world. Usually, the learner returns to an environment in which others have not had the benefits of such training and, accordingly, will not have developed the same skills and recipes of action and problem-solving. At the same time, any communication and interpersonal problems must be resolved by the parties themselves without recourse to a benevolent arbitrator concerned with their development.

This places an onus upon the returning learner to account for the feelings and problems of others. If a colleague lacks knowledge or skill this merely exposes a training need which the returning learner has been fortunate enough to address. The extension of sensitivity and empathy can be vital ways of addressing such issues.

- *What support is available to the learner?*

Whether the learner is trying to effect change within him or herself, or to tackle the problematic behaviour of others, he or she will almost certainly need some support. This is an area which is often overlooked, and one which can lead to the learner feeling vulnerable and likely to dismiss strategies and ideas as being too risky in a real-world situation, despite the fact that they were enthusiastically promoted on the training course.

Encourage learners to speak openly and honestly about support. Ask them to identify the characteristics of a support person and then to identify people around them who may have some or all of these qualities. At the same time, it might prove fruitful to open up the discussion in terms of support mechanisms and organizational structure. What responsibilities do managers have in this area? How likely is it that they will answer any call for support? Are there procedures and systems in place which are designed to support staff who challenge bad practice? The answers to these questions should not express undue optimism, but must address stark reality. It is of little use to argue that a person has a professional responsibility to extend support when the chips are down, if the reality is that he or she cannot, or will not.

In summary, learners may choose not to apply learning achieved on the course, or alternatively, may find their efforts to do so frustrated or hindered for one or more of the following reasons:

- Their efforts are unsupported by managers, friends, or colleagues.
- The ideas, strategies and ways of looking at and resolving problems that were developed on the course are found to be unrealistic and un-achievable in the real world.
- Insufficient account was taken of the differences between the effects of the training setting, with its safe and controlled environment, and the realities of the world outside the classroom.
- Others are unprepared for change resulting from the course and don't know how to react to it.
- Learners fail to apply new ways of working with others, and of thinking about and dealing with issues and problems, in a sensitive and careful manner.
- Learners were not really committed to the ideas and strategies developed on the course and quickly forget them, slipping back into the old way of doing things.
- No mechanism exists for reviewing learning and its application at a later stage.
- Others, who have not had similar training, remained bogged-down in old ways of thinking and are found to hamper progress.
- Insufficient regard was paid to the potential impact of the learner's real-world relationships and to his or her ability to effect necessary change or carry out planned action.

- Support for the learner is either ineffective or non-existent, or perhaps the question of support was not raised during training.

RECORDS OF LEARNERS' WORK

Almost from the start of any training course, learners will be committing their ideas to paper (often flipchart), and then sharing these ideas by 'publishing' them to the wider group. This material is extremely important and can often represent a written form of learning agenda that is referred to and expanded upon as the course develops (see Chapter 8).

It is particularly useful to attach early work, resulting from any issue or problem identification phases, to the walls of the course-room, not only to remind learners of this agenda, but also to facilitate the progress of that agenda with strategies and solutions which are generated in direct response to it as the course unfolds. We encourage learners to add their ideas and suggestions to a posted flipchart at any time that seems appropriate, thus ensuring that these contributions do not become lost or forgotten along the way.

By carefully utilizing the work that your learners produce, you will also enhance their individual ownership of the learning process, and through such acknowledgement, indicate the worth and usefulness of each learner's ideas and contributions. This written record can also chart the group's progress as they work through difficult and challenging issues, problems and experiences by allowing the facilitator to illustrate the development of their contributions at various stages of the course.

Learning requires the individual to reflect on the experiences that have occurred during training, to capture the meaning and significance of these experiences and their consequences for, and impact upon, previously held views and recipes for action and understanding. This is a fundamental part of the learning process, in which new ways of thinking, comprehending and behaving are compared with and validated against the person's existing knowledge and beliefs. This process of reflection, interpretation and validation will extend well beyond the course itself, and will include the learner's initial attempts at applying what has been learnt to real-world situations and problems. One way of assisting this ongoing reflective process is to provide learners with a written copy of their course work, structured in a comprehensive but accessible format. This has a peripheral benefit in that it represents a record of the ground covered and learning accomplished on the course, which can be provided to the course sponsor or organizer if required.

Pause for Thought

This pause for thought straddles two important facilitation issues, namely your use of learners' written work and the way in which you summarize key learning. Thinking about your current approach to facilitating learning:

- *In what way and to what extent do you make use of the written work produced by the learners on the courses you facilitate?*
- *How do you review the different learning phases of a course with the group?*
- *Do you provide a structured summary of key learning as part of course closure?*

SUMMARIZING KEY LEARNING

Summarizing progress, by referring to the written records of learners' contributions, is a good way of encouraging members of the group to consolidate learning. This is a vital part of the facilitator's role as the course nears its close, and the need to establish and maximize commitment to future action and necessary change increases. Learners need to be reminded of just how much they have achieved, and just how far their individual and group thinking has developed as a result of the training they have undertaken. All too often this summary is omitted, or is simply glossed over, and an ideal opportunity will have been missed to encourage everyone to carry this learning forward in to the real world.

This summarizing process will also help learners to understand how earlier parts of the course, which may have initially appeared unconnected or less relevant, eventually integrate to form a larger picture. There is, of course, no reason why such learning reviews should not occur as an ongoing part of the facilitative process, particularly where they provide an effective means of separating learning phases from one another. However, those summaries that mark the end of the training course have an additional strength, in that they enable both facilitator and learner alike to call upon and draw together each of the learning strands that were covered during the course.

Ideally, the summary of key learning, provided as part of course closure, should offer learners a structured opportunity to review important learning. To provide this, the facilitator must review both the learners' and his or her own learning notes, and should also reflect on significant phases and events. An *aide-memoire* containing useful questions can help prompt recall, and can

173

assist in providing a structure for reflections. We have provided a suggested set of questions which you could use for such a purpose:

- What was the course aim? Has it been realized? (Give examples).
- What were the planned learning outcomes? Have these been achieved? (Give examples).
- What problems arose between members of the group? Were these resolved? What learning came out of this? (Give examples).
- What was the level of effective disclosure and readiness to confront and address challenging issues and problems?
- What key issues, problems and experiences were identified at the outset as being pressing and significant to the group? (Give examples).
- To what extent were the real-world consequences of such problems, issues and experiences identified? (Give examples).
- How successful was the course in developing strategies, ideas and ways of thinking about and addressing such issues, experiences and problems? (Give examples).
- How realistic, useful and achievable are these ideas, strategies and new ways of thinking and behaving?
- Has the group been successful in identifying potential barriers to applying the things they have learnt on the course? Were strategies developed for overcoming or resisting such barriers?
- What real improvements are likely should learners fully apply things they have learnt on the course to the real world?

Figure 9.2 gives an overview of the main components of any effective review of key learning. As with all other aspects of Real-world Facilitation, it will prove to be of most value to the learning process if done systematically. Summarizing key learning is an important aspect of course closure and should ideally be a two-way process, providing both facilitator and learners the opportunity to share with the learning group their views and feelings as to the effectiveness of the course, and what they felt had been achieved at a personal level. As with any other learning phase, this part of the course should be active, and should be appropriately structured so as to allow sufficient opportunity for necessary personal and group reflection. It is worth remembering that the length of time it will take to summarize key learning is in direct proportion to the amount of work that has been done on the course. During a course of five working days for example, it would not be unreasonable to devote the whole of the last afternoon to this phase.

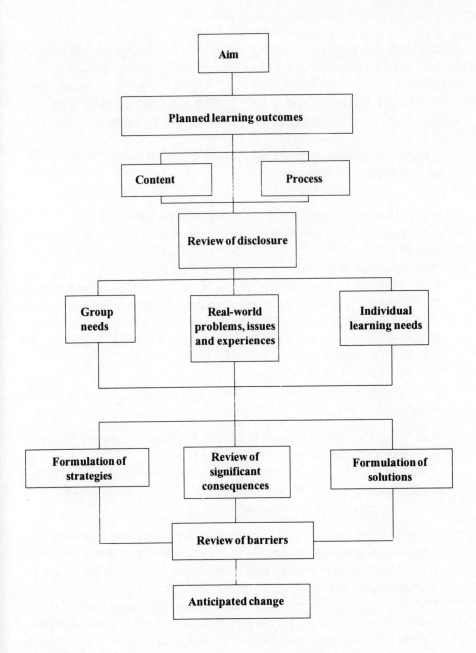

Figure 9.2 *A systematic approach to reviewing the key learning in a course*

COURSE CLOSURE

Always try to end your course or training session on a high note. Remember that now is not the time to deal with questions majoring on the potential barriers that learners might face when trying to transfer and apply their learning. This is the time for closing remarks and statements of commitment from the learners, to take their learning from the training environment into their real world.

To maximize learner commitment to transferring the things learnt on the course to the world of everyday life, this final learning activity could include challenging questions such as:

- What has been the most important learning on the course for you?
- What parts of the course will be particularly useful to you in your real world?
- How do you plan to make use of the things you have learnt?
- What problems or issues do you feel you have resolved on this course?
- Do you consider that you have acquired new skills on this course; if so what are these skills and how will they be of use to you?
- How will you ensure that the hard work you have invested in this course doesn't go to waste?
- Has the course challenged or changed your viewpoint on the issues we have worked through? If so, how will this change affect your future behaviour?

We have found it to be quite useful at this stage to give the learners free rein and to receive their remarks without further comment.

In addition to summarizing and consolidating the learning that has taken place and focusing learner attention towards it application, closure can also serve other important needs; for example:

- Rewarding members of the group for their hard work and contributions. Even though you may have actively rewarded learners throughout their time with you, a final encouraging word during the close of the course is an important part of keeping enthusiasm and resolve high.
- Allowing your learners to congratulate themselves and each other. If the course has been challenging and participants have worked hard and contributed well, they may need space at the end of the course to admit these facts to themselves and to fellow group members, and to applaud a job well done.
- Ensuring that the course doesn't simply fizzle out. The end of the course should mark a point of transition from training to application, and the

motivation and impetus that has characterized work on the course should follow the learner into the real world where possible.

- Allowing learners to acknowledge the bonds that have formed between them, and to say goodbye to the group, the members of which may not meet again. Even on relatively short courses, learners may form friendships and bonds with others, particularly on those courses which have involved significant self-disclosure and the resolution of challenging and difficult issues.

REAL-WORLD FACILITATION: SOME CONCLUDING REMARKS

Increasingly, people are beginning to realize the true potential of facilitation as an effective method of teaching which has demonstrated the capacity to encourage lasting learning. Learners appreciate the active and experiential style of this work and the safe and conducive environment in which it takes place. Trainers enjoy its challenges and rewards and believe in the validity of a method which seeks out and utilizes learners' contributions as a central theme. Sponsors understand its significance as an effective means of confronting and addressing complex attitudinal and interpersonal problems and issues.

But at the very time when facilitation is growing in both popularity and acceptability, it has begun to falter, and now threatens to lose its way. The adoption of any one of a number of extreme approaches has resulted in a dilution of early rigour and discipline which characterized this valuable educational approach. Whether needs-led or neutral, mechanical or psychotherapeutic, facilitation is increasingly being called into question, or is stigmatized as 'alternative-teaching'.

We firmly believe that Real-world Facilitation can rescue the integrity of this teaching style, by providing a facilitative model which, while remaining true to the fundamental facilitative precepts of learner-centred, activity-based, experiential learning, extends and enhances them by concentrating their focus on those methods and techniques by which effective and long-lasting learning is maximized. It is a coherent and comprehensive model of teaching which emphasizes the need to place issues of learner relevance, significance and meaning centre-stage.

When individuals enter a learning environment and begin the process of listening, thinking and reflecting, they become engaged in a constant attempt to capture the meaning of what is being said and done. This is an ongoing process in which the learners try to link in any new information or behaviour with the things they 'know' or understand to be the case already, ie, links with their own experience, knowledge and understanding. Our model constantly and systematically strives to bridge the divide between theory and practice, classroom and workplace, and between new and existing knowledge and experience. Accordingly, it greatly assists the learner in the fundamental process of establishing these necessary links, which ultimately make learning meaningful, enhancing its retention and maximizing the likelihood of its application.

At the same time, Real-world Facilitation demands a pragmatic approach to ideas, strategies, and solutions that are offered by learners themselves in the course of their training. Our approach requires that such contributions should be tested and validated to ascertain whether they are achievable, realistic and useful in the very setting where they will eventually be applied. Failure to do this will render training impotent, relegating it to the level of a talking shop, in which ideas remain just that – ideas! Real-world Facilitation is about learning for living. Try it – your learners will thank you for it and you will experience the sheer joy of helping others to learn.

References

Ausubel, D P, Novak, J S and Hanesian, H (1978) *Educational Psychology: A Cognitive View* (2nd ed), New York: Holt, Rinehart and Winston.

Boshear, W and Albrecht, K (1977) *Understanding People: Models and Concepts,* California: University Associates.

Boud, D (1988) *Developing Student Autonomy in Learning,* London: Kogan Page.

Brookfield, S D (1991) *Understanding and Facilitating Adult Learning,* Milton Keynes: Open University Press.

Brundage, D H and Mackeracher, D (1980) *Adult Learning Principles and their Application to Program Planning,* Ontario: Ministry of Education.

Buzan, T (1989) *Use Your Head,* London: BBC Books.

Curzon, L B (1990) *Teaching in Further Education* (4th edn), London: Cassell.

Heron, J (1977) *Dimensions of Facilitator Style,* Guildford: Human Potential Resource Group, University of Surrey.

Heron, J (1989) *Six Category Intervention Analysis,* Guildford: Human Potential Resource Group, University of Surrey.

Heron, J (1989) *The Facilitator's Handbook,* London: Kogan Page.

Kolb, D (1975) 'Towards an applied theory of experimental learning', in Cooper C L (ed.) *Theories of Group Processes,* Chichester: Wiley.

Mager, R F (1984) *Preparing Instructional Objectives,* California: Pitman Belmont.

Marton, F and Säljö, R (1976a) 'On qualitative differences in learning: I.

Outcome and process', *British Journal of Educational Psychology,* **46,** 4–11.

Marton, F and Säljö, R (1976b) 'On qualitative differences in learning: II. Outcome as a function of the learner's conception of the task', *British Journal of Educational Psychology,* **46,** 115–27.

Marton, F and Säljö, R (1984) 'Approaches to learning', in Marton, F, Hounsell, D and Entwistle, N J (eds) *The Experiences of Learning,* Edinburgh: Scottish Academic Press, pp. 36–55.

Schutz, A (1962, 1964, 1966) *Collected Papers,* Volumes I, II and III, The Hague: Martinus Nijhoff.

Tessmer, M and Harris, D (1992) *Analysing the Instructional Setting,* London: Kogan Page.

INDEX